BUMPING BACK

AN ACTIVIST'S GUIDE TO GETTING THERE, DOING THE BUSINESS AND GETTING AWAY WITH IT

by L Hobley

BUMPING BACK

AN ACTIVIST'S GUIDE TO GETTING THERE, DOING THE BUSINESS AND GETTING AWAY WITH IT

L. HOBLEY

NICCOLO PRESS

"The state calls its own violence law, but that of the individual crime."
Max Stirner

ISBN 978 0 944061 16 5

BUMPING BACK is published by
Niccolo Press
Lima, Ohio, USA

DISCLAIMER

The content of this book is for information only. It must only be read by responsible persons over the age of 18. Many of the techniques described are dangerous or illegal and frequently both and should therefore never be used.

WARNING!

The publisher assumes no responsibilities for any misuse of the information presented in this book. Serious harm or death could occur from attempting to perform any of the methods in this publication. This book and the information contained herein are merely presented for reading enjoyment and entertainment, and is not intended for actual use!

  The publisher does not take any responsibility for your actions. Furthermore the publisher wants to make clear that we have no connection at all with the writer(s) of this book. The publisher will not be held responsible for damages, loss or anything else arising from the use of the information provided in this book.

This book is dedicated to the children
who will grow up to bump back.

... we shall go
Always a little further: it may be
Beyond that last blue mountain barred with snow
Across that angry or that glimmering sea.
(James Elroy Flecker)

Contents

Introduction 11

Part One
Bumping Back 15
From Thought to Action 17
Leadership 23
The Way of the Warrior? 25
Violence 27
Weapons 29
How Far Will You Go? 31
Terrorist, Who's a Terrorist? 33

Part Two
Preparing for the Party 35
Forensics 37
Security 43
Pre-Action 45
On the Ground 47
Rendezvous (RVs) and Emergency Rendezvous (ERVs) 52
Vehicles 55
Disguises 58
If it All Goes King Kong 61

Part Three
The Party 63
Checklist for Recces/Actions 67
Defeating Security 71
Gone to the Dogs 75
Burglary 77

Part Four
Party Tricks 83
Navigation 86
Barriers 97
First Aid 101
Climbing 113
Tree Stirruping 116

Prussiking 117
Fitness 123
Self Defence 128
Survival Techniques 133

Part Five
Party Games 135
Individual Camouflage and Concealment 137
Urban Camouflage 139
Rural Camouflage 141
Winter Camouflage 144
Equipment Camouflage and Concealment 146
Night Work 147
Night Walking 151
How to Walk Silently at Night 152
Movement to Target Area 154
Movement Security 156
Packing 157
Arm-and-Hand Signals 158
Route Selection 159
Ministry of Silly Walks 161
Hearing 163
Smell 165
Avoid Being Smelled 166
Sleep 169
How to Build a Poncho/Basha Hooch 171
Night Time Signals 173
Reconnaissance 175
Hides and Surveillance Sites 177
Single Person Surveillance 182
Escape and Evasion 185
Urban Escape and Evasion 188
Tracking and Counter Tracking 191
How They May Find Us 196
The Vehicle Question 199

Part Six
After the Party 209
Post-Action 211
Post-Action Training 213

You Have Already Made a Difference 214

Glossary 219

Useful Sources 223

Appendix i
The Phonetic Alphabet 227

Appendix ii
Equipment: NVGs, Thermal Imaging, etc. 229

Appendix iii
Forensics 235

Introduction

I have been involved in direct action in one form or another for a long time. I have seen enthusiasm for activism wax and wane; tactics evolve and the libertarian/anarchist/autonomous movement reinvent itself several times. The causes taken up by activists have changed too, from intervening in industrial struggles, to being rowdy on the fringes of the anti-nuclear movement, through to the current involvement in environmental and anti-globalisation issues.

Recent technological 'advances' have enabled the state to increase its surveillance to near omniscient levels but then, arguably, many of the anti-globalisation actions could not have taken place without the almost instant communication afforded by the internet.

One constant is that every group seems to start from scratch in terms of organisation and, while people certainly can learn from their own mistakes, it can be a very costly learning process. It's much better overall to learn from someone else's mistakes. To this end read *Direct Action* by Ann Hansen. Learn how not to set fire to yourself.

It was largely due to reading an excellent article in *Do or Die* called 'Action Stations' (parts of which have been incorporated into the text), which prompted me to look at reappraising some of the tactics of direct action. *Bumping Back* is the result. It is also the sort of book I would have liked to have read when I first started out to annoy the state. Its intention is to put forward some practical ideas on how to tactically approach a target and conduct surveillance without being seen yourself, how to approach and leave a target during an action and, if it all goes wrong, how to escape. Along the way are Top Tips, essential skills, pointers towards extending your skills base, a bit of politics and really bad puns.

This is not an urban guerrilla manual, but I believe that by adopting a more systematic approach you can:
- improve the way you go about the planning of actions;
- increase the overall efficiency of your actions by having a systematic method of planning and conducting them;
- increase the chances of pulling off a successful action and, perhaps most importantly;
- lessen the chances of getting busted.

As far as I am aware this is the only comprehensive 'how to' manual for activists in the UK. It is needed, particularly in the English speaking countries, because we do not have, amongst the modern, specifically anarchist/autonomous movement, a history of highly organised and effective activist resistance. The activities of the Angry Brigade are the only examples I can think of in the UK.

This is not intended as an aspirational document but rather as a practical guide presenting some suggestions for the organisation of your group. You may not choose to use these techniques at the moment but there is no reason why you can't gear up to using them in the future and you can start practicing most of the tactics advocated in the book now. You don't have to buy costly clothing or equipment to wander about the hills building hides and getting lost. And you can have some great fun playing tracking and surveillance games which increase confidence in your abilities and develop trust and camaraderie within the group. You may think that your group is not big enough to take on these tasks but you only need two or three people to be effective. (Look what Castro achieved: him and half a dozen of his mates, after a night on the rum, was all it took to start a revolution, overthrow a dictator, get rid of the Mafia and seriously piss off the Yanks for half a century.) You may think, at first sight, that some of the tactics are too sophisticated. Look again, everything has been explained, starting from the absolute basics and if your average teenage squaddie can get their head round them, then you can too. Ah! The military. The fact that some of the techniques are used by our opponents does not mean that they should not be used by us. After all, the methods described have been tried and tested by insurgents and activists the world over. And if you don't like the language please feel free to bowdlerise this as much as you like for use with your own group.

You may feel that your group doesn't have the time to put these tactics into practice. That's fine if the action is minor and the risks and consequences small, but if your group embarks upon a serious project, I think the motto should be 'find the time or do the time'. We already have too many comrades inside and it's not just that – sure it's no big deal getting a fine (after all the movement will pay), or spending a few days or months in the nick. But what is a big deal, you are giving the cops your DNA, which may end up being the only evidence which convicts you of a serious 'crime' in years to come; you are alerting the cops to your involvement in political action and as a corollary tipping them off to the presence of an active group on their patch.

There is also a section on escape and evasion which covers how you might be tracked after completion of an action (or if you are sussed before completion). I think it is important to understand the tactics that may be employed against you in order to avoid them. To this end I have included notes on what police dogs and their handlers will be looking for. I have tried to keep the text as jargon free as possible, although I think a certain amount is inevitably going to creep in – this is not necessarily a bad thing as it does help you to be more concise in detailing and explaining your plans if you all know what you are talking about when you use a certain word or phrase. I have tried to make these notes coherent and logically sequential but there will certainly be a crossover of information, so it may be necessary to flip backwards and forwards to find the bits you need.

Use the information progressively; don't be daunted by it, and, before you know it, using the techniques will become second nature. This is a guide to planning the most extreme actions your group is ever likely to undertake but it is very easy to scale it down, adapt it and indeed use it for purposes other than planning an action.

There are sections which are personal and opinionated, probably politically incorrect in some circles, and I would certainly be surprised if everything is to your taste. But if you are an anarchist and it pisses you off, that's great, write your own.

I'm sure there are other techniques used by activists to get the job done and plenty of Top Tips. Circulate them on the net.

You will notice a large number of quotes scattered through the text. They are there because they are relevant or inspirational and I hope they will serve as an antidote to the insularity engendered by a literary diet of dry political works and meeting speak. Broadening your outlook will, to quote one of my favourite books, help you become 'dangerous men' and women.

> "All men dream: but not equally. Those who dream by night in the dusty recesses of their minds wake in the day to find that it was vanity: but the dreamers of the day are dangerous men, for they may act their dreams with open eyes, to make it possible. This I did." (T.E. Lawrence, *Seven Pillars of Wisdom*).

PART ONE

BUMPING

BACK

"In the absence of light, darkness prevails. There are things that go bump in the night, Agent Myers. Make no mistake about that. And we are the ones who bump back." (Professor Trevor 'Broom' Bruttenholm, *Hellboy*).

Part One contains practical hints, philosophical musings, politics, morals, sex and violence … and that's just part one.

From Thought to Action

ORCHESTRAL MANOEUVRES IN THE DARK, A BUTTERFLY BARES ITS TEETH.

"You're obliged to pretend respect for people and institutions you think absurd. You live attached in a cowardly fashion to moral and social conventions you despise, condemn, and know lack all foundation. It is that permanent contradiction between your ideas and desires and all the dead formalities and vain pretences of your civilisation which makes you sad, troubled and unbalanced. In that intolerable conflict you lose all joy of life and all feeling of personality, because at every moment they suppress and restrain and check the free play of your powers. That's the poisoned and mortal wound of the civilised world." (Octave Mirbeau, *The Torture Garden*)

You are not the only one who has sat listening to the news, fists clenched, guts knotted in inchoate rage but with an urge to action rushing up your spine. You want to lash out, strike a blow against the global capitalist machine which is crushing the life force out of the planet and its inhabitants. But where do you start, what should be your target – the machine seems so massive, what possible effect could you have against it? Let's assume that before you drown in a sea of negativity, you manage to propel yourself to the surface and hurl yourself into the fray. Your confidence grows and you start to experience the savage joy of destruction. You become an artist, you compose, conduct and perform symphonies in shattered glass with the oppressors' windows as instruments; you combine literature and fine art with your graffiti. But it is still not enough. What you have created may have been virtuoso performances but you are still a soloist and you now want to join the orchestra.

We truly believe that even though we live in an evil world, if you can stand up with a stronger will, then you can't be beaten down – John Woo

THE STRING QUARTET

We are some way off from performing orchestral works on the concert platform of the world and anyway, at the moment, the pieces you want to play are best performed by a string quartet.

AFFINITY GROUPS

Affinity groups have always been a part of anarchist organisation. If you use the techniques in *Bumping Back* they are vital, as trust, common training and security are at the heart of all these notes. The further you get into anti-state naughtiness, the more pressure will be brought to bear to squash you. And the more compellingly attractive the entreaties to members of 'the movement' to give you up will become. It may come as a surprise to you but there are people within our movement who are quite happily churning out shelves of incomprehensible books and producing turgid articles for dreary magazines as their contribution to the struggle. There are others who go on the odd demo and talk it up at dinner parties. But when these types of people have their flats raided, get threatened by the bill and generally have their risk averse lifestyle put in jeopardy they will start first to criticise you in print, denouncing you as adventurist and the like and then they will begin naming names. It has happened before and it is even more likely

> **To the uneducated, an A is just three sticks** – Winnie the Pooh

to happen now. They may call it pragmatism for the good of the movement. I call it grassing.

As the potential consequences of being busted before, during or after an action increase, the more important it is for the development of a cellular structure to your affinity group, which itself nestles within the larger movement. This book is written from an anarchist perspective so don't expect to see references (unless derogatory) to political commissars or vanguards or cadres.

The affinity group is just that; people with an affinity for each other and for a certain way of working; a group bound together by common endeavour, who are in agreement on targets and tactics and have the capacity to work constructively and cooperatively. The closer the bonds, the less likely people are to give up other members of the group and the more you will risk for your mates. As to the operators on a particular action; you must be as close as possible. Think of it like this; there will always be people in the group who, even though they share exactly your ideals, you find irritating, too domineering, too dogmatic. Whatever. You may find that with these people your instinct for survival may be more dominant than your desire to protect a comrade. You cannot afford for this to happen, so don't work with them on anything too sensitive.

GROUP GENESIS

Any hard core activist group will grow and develop as new members are brought in. It is a natural process as existing members invite trusted friends to join. The group needs to be a certain size to enable a diverse range of available skills and talents; a pool from which to draw the constituent parts of a viable hit squad. But the group must not be allowed to grow too large or it will reach critical mass, where maintaining effective security becomes impossible.

PSYCHOLOGICAL FITNESS

The life of an activist can be a very stressful one. There is always the constant fear of arrest. And maintaining security means that you always refrain from discussing the actions you have taken part in, even with non-participating members of your own group. As you up the ante with the seriousness of your actions, all information is shared on a strictly need to know basis – so no bragging down the pub. While developing the hit squad element within the group (starting with low risk, low skill operations and building up) it should be possible to gauge an individual's capacity to soak up the stress and manage the paranoia.

Some of the revolutionary direct action groups of the '70s became completely isolated from the larger 'movement'. They were totally wrapped up in the fight and believed themselves to be superior because they had sacrificed their lives to attacking the State. But bear in mind this…

"Wer mit Ungeheuern kampft, mag zusehn,
daß er nicht dabei zum Ungeheuer wird.
Und wenn du lange in einen Abgrund blickst,
blickt der Abgrund auch in dich hinein."
(Friedrich Nietzsche, *Jenseits von Gut und Bose IV 146*)
(*He who fights with monsters should look to it that he himself does not become a monster ... when you gaze long into the abyss, the abyss also gazes into you.*)

SPOTTING THE INFILTRATORS

A group I was involved with used to regularly play 'spot the infiltrator', the most likely culprit changed from month to month. We never found one. But that doesn't mean anything. Certainly many groups have been taken in by infiltrators, so check the pedigree of new members thoroughly. Be wary of the super gung ho, it could be a sign that they are agents provocateurs. One member could have a grudge against another member of the group – sexual jealousy has probably destroyed more tightly knit groups than political or tactical differences. Or someone might have been busted and turned by the cops. Don't get paranoid, just be careful.

> Piglet was still a little anxious about Tigger, who was a very Bouncy Animal, with a way of saying How-do-you-do which always left your ears full of sand
> – Winnie the Pooh

POLITICS, POLITICS

> "A dogma is a man's best friend." (The Author, *Drunken Aphorisms*)

DOGMAS, HOWEVER COMFORTING, PREVENT YOU FROM THINKING, OSSIFY YOUR POLITICAL DEVELOPMENT AND CAN BE DISASTROUS IN A GROUP.

The longevity and cohesiveness of an activist group is achieved and maintained by the actions themselves. The esprit de corps and camaraderie engendered by training and facing danger together are very powerful and are similar to the deep and long lasting bonds forged during wartime.

> People who don't think probably don't have brains; rather, they have grey fluff that's blown into their heads by mistake – Winnie the Pooh

These bonds are formed not by adherence to a particular ideology but by common endeavour. This is where an activist group scores big time over a traditional political group and its factionalism. An activist group will, of course, have established very broad objectives e.g. 'an end to animal exploitation'.

And from there will go on to develop strategies and tactics which will aim it towards that outcome. That is all you need. Nowhere is there a need for a textual analysis of the works of long dead theorists to discover their position on the treatment of pit ponies in the nineteenth century and from that be able to extrapolate what the party line on vivisection should be.

"During the years in which the women's liberation movement has been taking shape, a great emphasis has been placed on what are called leaderless, structureless groups as the main – if not sole – organisational form of the movement. The source of this idea was a natural reaction against the over-structured society in which most of us found ourselves, the inevitable control this gave others over our lives, and the continual elitism of the Left and similar groups among those who were supposedly fighting this overstructuredness." (Jo Freeman, *The Tyranny of Structurelessness*)

This is not a plea for political illiteracy. I'm sure that the people you invite into your group will be politically sussed and have a thorough understanding of the issues you intend to tackle. They should have an ideological maturity gained through working with other groups and will probably have come to your group out of a frustration with not having been able to see a quantifiable, positive difference in the world brought about by the previous actions they have taken part in. It should also be made clear within your group that, even though it is highly unlikely and probably undesirable that all the members will have identical political beliefs, there is no room in a libertarian group like yours for racism, sexism, macho posturing and authoritarianism. These tendencies must always be challenged, even if that means losing an otherwise valuable member of the group.

Leadership

> "We can't all, and some of us don't. That's all there is." (Winnie the Pooh)

As has been noted above, every effort should be made to combat authoritarian behaviour within the group, but authoritarianism is not the same as leadership. The idea of having a 'leader' is something you are going to instinctively baulk at. But it is something you are going to have to come to terms with if you genuinely want your actions to succeed.

The concept of leadership is certainly not unknown within the libertarian tradition, from undoubted leaders such as Nestor Makhno who commanded an insurrectionary army in the Ukraine through to the elected officers of the anarchist fighting columns during the Spanish Civil War.

A leader should not be a ruler but rather someone we have confidence in to make decisions under stressful conditions. For example if you were somewhere on the Ben Nevis plateau, in a whiteout, almost zero visibility, gale force winds making it barely possible to stand, sub-zero temperatures and surrounded by the very real threat of avalanche, then you would be a fool if you would not welcome an expert in that environment to make the important decisions and lead you.

Similarly, when the mob-handed arrival of the cops is imminent, it is not the time to call a meeting, weigh up the pros and cons of every possible action and eventually arrive at a consensus on what to do next. It is, rather, the time when you look to the leader you have chosen for this particular action to come up with the best way out of the situation.

If you are lucky your group will have more than one person suitable to act as a leader on actions but it is impossible to tell who they will be until they are tested. To this end, training, the more realistic and stressful the better, can often show who will not be a good leader and the results may be surprising. Depending on the action you will need different leadership qualities. It may be a situation where you need an expert navigator or one where a high level of electronic or mechanical skills is more appropriate. The training sessions will help you sort out who can hold it together, make decisions, effectively communicate those decisions and use their expertise while under enormous levels of stress. These are the leaders.

QUALITIES OF LEADERSHIP

The leader does not have to be a master strategist. They must have a comprehensive understanding of the plan and the 'actions on' that will have been worked up by the group as a whole. It is in a crisis situation that a leader comes into their own. It is the ability to process information from multiple sources; what they can see and hear themselves; radio traffic; what is being relayed to them by other group members, and to synthesise it into an immediate action plan that they are able to communicate effectively, which goes towards defining a leader. Speed and decisiveness are the crucial factors which could mean the difference between getting away with it and ending up in jail.

The leader's immediate action plan might not be perfect and post action, over a couple of pints, it might be possible to devise a better one. But it is the capacity, while at the sharp end, to come up with a viable instant solution to the problem at hand that is important. It is, however imperfect, infinitely better than charging around like headless chickens waiting to be nicked.

For situations where an immediate action plan must be formed quickly but not instantly, the 'Chinese parliament' model should be followed. This is where all the people involved at the time make suggestions and the leader chooses the one they think the most likely to succeed.

The Way of the Warrior?

"The Way of a Warrior is based on humanity, love, and sincerity; the heart of martial valour is true bravery, wisdom, love, and friendship. Emphasis on the physical aspects of warriorship is futile, for the power of the body is always limited." (Ueshiba Morihei, *The Art Of Peace*)

The previous chapter called for a re-evaluation of the concept of leadership. I would like to address in this chapter the (probably easier) concept and role of the Warrior in a direct action context. The task is probably easier because activists are at least used to seeing the word in a hyphenated sense (Eco-warrior, etc.). But again a plea, to suspend your knee-jerk reactions to the connotations of the word itself and have a look at what we might choose it to mean.

From the martial to the mystical, the warrior has, throughout history, been seen as an individual with the capacity to focus on the task in hand and see it through to the end.

WE ARE ALL SPARTACUS

There is no room in the warrior for machismo or vainglory. This type of posturing is the antithesis of focus. The warrior learns to calm their mind and increase their awareness.

In a stressful situation powerful hormones flood the body and one of their effects is to create a type of tunnel vision where your consciousness is concentrated narrowly and solely on an imminent danger or perceived threat, to the exclusion of the plethora of available information surrounding you. You can therefore only respond to the stimuli emanating from the end of your adrenalin-manufactured tunnel.

The opposite of the 'tunnel vision syndrome' is when you are incapable of coping with the overwhelming flood of information coming your way. This is, of course, happening at precisely the time when you need to be able to instantly filter out the extraneous and concentrate on the important; to categorise and assign values to sensory input and get on with the action.

THE WARRIOR MOMENT

So it all comes down to focus. There are many techniques the warrior can utilise to develop focus, from meditation to breathing control. Teaching these techniques is beyond the scope of this book. But for inspiration just look in any 'remaindered' bookshop and you will find literally hundreds of titles in the Self

Help, Yoga, Tai Chi, and Martial Arts sections that claim to teach the techniques to transform you into a warrior. There is no reason why everyone in the group shouldn't go down the path to becoming a warrior. See it as a concept which is on a sliding scale and go as far as you want or think useful.

THE CHALLENGE

Becoming a warrior is one of the most effective ways of coping with the extreme pressure you will be put under whilst bumping back. And even though I could go on at great length expostulating my theories on warriorship, they are likely to be little more than a rehash of what has been said far more eloquently by warriors from Sun Tzu to Winnie the Pooh.

Here is a small selection of quotes on the way of the warrior, beginning with this warning to George W. Bush:

> "Chaos is born from order.
> Cowardice is born from bravery.
> Weakness is born from strength."
> (Sun Tzu)

> "To achieve the mood of a warrior is not a simple matter. It is a revolution. To regard the lion and the water rats and our fellow men as equals is a magnificent act of a warrior's spirit. It takes power to do that."
> (Carlos Castaneda)
>
> "Whenever you meet difficult situations dash forward bravely and joyfully."
> (Tsunetomo Yamamoto, *Hagakure*)
>
> "I am a Shawnee. My forefathers were warriors. Their son is a warrior ... From my tribe I take nothing. I am the maker of my own fortune."
> (Tecumseh)
>
> "Courageous, untroubled, mocking and violent – that is what Wisdom wants us to be. Wisdom is a woman, and loves only a warrior."
> (Friedrich Nietzsche)

Violence

"There comes a time in every man's life when he's consumed by the desire to spit on his palms, hoist the black flag and start cutting throats." (Henry Louis Mencken)

The next couple of pages on violence and weapons may make you feel uncomfortable but it would be dishonest if your group did not address both topics seriously and preferably with an open mind.

Unfortunately the chapters on Sex, Drugs and Rock 'n' Roll have been omitted due to space constraints.

'DID SOMEONE SAY VIOLENCE?'

It has already been noted that not every member of your group will be suited for every action and that everyone should have the courage to say when they are not up for a particular action. The group should be able to support various ideas, temperaments and dispositions but, and it is a really big 'but', I don't think there can be any place in an activist group for someone who would describe themselves as a pacifist. So with the battle cry 'alienate the moderates' ringing in the air, get rid of the pacifists – they will get in the way, let you down and end up getting you busted. This is not just rhetoric. I have had the misfortune to work with pacifists in the past and they really are a liability. They will stand by denouncing police violence without doing anything to help their comrades who are getting the shit kicked out of them.

BULLY BOYS AND GIRLS NEED NOT APPLY

By the same token there is absolutely no place in the group for someone who glorifies violence and tries to indulge in it at every opportunity. It is likely to be damaging to them and probably to the group as a whole. Of course context is everything and it is wise, as a group, to set the parameters within which violence is an acceptable tactic and where walking, or running, away is the best policy.

The extent of any violence you use also has to be determined by the group as a whole and any 'rules of engagement' must be strictly adhered to. Individuals will lose trust in the group if they find themselves in a situation where there is a level of violence being used which had not been discussed and agreed upon beforehand.

VIOLENCE, VANGUARDISM AND THE PEOPLE

I think it has been made clear enough that this book has nothing to do with vanguardism and indeed anyone reading this who is of that persuasion, just put it down now, it will do you no good. Anyone who thinks that they are in the van of anything and that using this book will further their aims, is just a self-deluded fool. If you use violence you will be denounced by 'the people,' even if many of them broadly support your cause, and probably by many in 'the movement' as well. There will be no popular uprising that you can lead and the people will not take up the struggle.

Violence should only be used either tactically, in the service of a strategic objective, or to get yourself or others out of a mess. Of course, it is always okay to give Nazis a good slapping. And remember:

> "The state calls its own violence law, but that of the individual crime." (Max Stirner)

Weapons

"The strongest reason for the people to retain the right to keep and bear arms is, as a last resort, to protect themselves against tyranny in government." (Thomas Jefferson)

The American constitution was drawn up by a bunch of revolutionaries, bourgeois revolutionaries to be sure, but revolutionaries none the less. The much discussed but poorly understood, constitutional right to bear arms is a revolutionary principle. Its whole basis is that the people should always have the right to form militia to overthrow unjust governments. This is of course the last thing the state wants and indeed there have been significant curbs on gun ownership in the States, not least the outlawing of fully automatic weapons – the weapons carried by the army who, presumably, will be the ones standing between the militias and the tyrannical government.

HAPPINESS IS A WARM GUN

In a book like this it would be at best disingenuous to discuss all this other stuff and somehow neglect to mention weapons. By starting this piece with the US it would seem that I have closed off any possibility of discussion. After all, don't the statistics for gunshot deaths alone preclude any sensible debate on the pros and cons of gun possession. I don't know. But certainly the statistics should be given more than a cursory glance. Gun deaths in the US do not have an even geographical spread. In fact there are many areas, usually rural, where gun ownership is close to 100% by household but there is very little evidence of people using those guns on each other. However, what really skews the stats are the pockets in the inner city areas of all the major urban centres where gun deaths are incredibly high. Looking closer we see areas of massive deprivation where the killing of deprived, mainly black youth is done by other deprived, mainly black youth. It would be patronising to attempt explanations for why this might be. If the guns did not exist I think it is reasonable to assume that the killings would continue by other means. The really tragic consequence of gun use – rather than the use of say, machetes – is that there are plenty of unintended victims of stray bullets. Canada, just an arbitrary line on a map away does not have significant gun deaths – discuss.

...THEY DO THINGS DIFFERENTLY THERE

In Europe things are very different. Switzerland still has National Service and every 18 year old male is required to spend time in the army. Thereafter they have to keep their weapon and do annual rifle practice. So every house in Switzerland with an over-18 male resident is also a house containing a fully automatic weapon. We don't hear a lot about shootings in Switzerland – that's because there aren't any. We also don't hear a lot about massive inner city deprivation in Switzerland.

BLAME IT ON THE REDS

In the UK, anti-gun legislation was very blatantly political. It occurred in the aftermath of the first world war, when the government was absolutely cacking itself at the thought of millions of very pissed off, weapons trained, young men coming home from the hell of the trenches to the hell of post-war poverty. That, coupled with the fear that these young men might have been infected with dangerous, insurrectionary ideas from the Russian revolution of the previous year, made it imperative that these boys were disarmed.

'YOU CALL THAT A KNIFE?'

I suppose we should have some definition of what a weapon is. We could say that a weapon is anything you use to cause harm. As we will see in the self-defence section almost everything can be used as a weapon, so it is not going to be easy (possible?) for the group to come up with an intelligent policy on the subject of weapons and their use or non-use. But as with all the other issues we have discussed, everyone in the group should be aware of everyone else's parameters regarding the use of weapons, including what weapons to use and in what circumstances they will be used.

How Far Will You Go?

"Whoever will be free must make himself free. Freedom is no fairy gift to fall into a man's lap. What is freedom? To have the will to be responsible for one's self." (Max Stirner)

MORALS AND OBSCENITIES

Anarchists do not believe that the ends justify the means. We believe that the two cannot be separated. We need to be really clear about this. It cannot be justifiable to do something which is morally indefensible in order to achieve, perhaps, at a later date, one of our goals. Collateral damage, those obscene words devised to be hidden behind by politicians when they are talking about the murder of innocent civilians, is not an option.

How could we condemn the state for hurting innocents if we do the same ourselves? Everything in this book is written with that as a fundamental principle. It is easy to comprehend the frustration, anger and bitterness of someone who has had their homeland stolen or who has suffered all their lives from prejudice or discrimination but we should still condemn them if their idea of getting back at their oppressors is to leave a bomb on a bus packed with working class men, women and children.

As I sipped my whisky looking over the beach and white flashes of surf into the darkness over the ocean, it was hard to believe it had all happened. The elations and terrors of this long, hot day washed over me, like the relentless waves breaking on the sand, and I felt a stunning disbelief that I had really survived. The delicious sense of composure I experienced after I had recovered from that really bad moment with myself was still with me. Exposure to extreme danger for so long – and time is always the essential ingredient in this priceless annealing of the mind and character – had produced an exquisite sense of detachment which allowed me to savour every aspect and tiny detail of what I had been doing. Even - and especially - the bad parts. Post-combat trauma … has no place in this calm and rarefied state in which the mind has been improved and strengthened by the experience, expanded and empowered by the extreme tensions. This was strength of spirit, amounting to faith, like steel hardened in fire. I had never felt better. (Will Scully, *Once A Pilgrim*)

PARAMETERS NOT PARADIGMS

Each individual activist must define their own moral parameters and stick to them and not be coerced or bullied into an action which they consider to be morally indefensible. You alone can decide what length you are prepared to go to, to achieve your objective. When you have got that sussed you should look at any proposed action to see if it fits within your moral framework. If it does not, you can either lobby to modify the action or sit it out.

The group members need to have respect for each other and not apply peer pressure, no matter how subtle, to get someone to go along with the wishes of the majority – this in not a democracy: the tyranny of the majority is, after all, tyranny.

Be open and flexible. If your beliefs do not change over time, check your pulse, you are probably dead. It is quite natural for you to now adhere to beliefs and to hold a moral position you thought was extreme a couple of years ago (or vice versa). What is not acceptable in an activist group is moral ambivalence. Take a stand.

MANIFESTOS AND COMMUNIQUÉS

Detailed manifestos are usually a bad idea. They presuppose a very precise ideology and political direction, which should be anathema to an activist group. The group needs the fluidity to change as events unfold. It should not be bound by the inflexibility of manifestos.

Any communiqués issued by the group should be clear and jargon free and without the taint of vanguardist ego-tripping.

A concise communiqué would be along the lines of 'the target does this – it is bad because of this – we gave the target a slap – we will do it again'. The group can sign with a particular name, or a generic one a la the Angry Brigade, or it can be anonymous.

Terrorist! Who's a Terrorist?

Well you possibly. Animal rights activists, roads protesters and it seems just about anyone who disagrees with the state gets branded a terrorist by the government and its press.

All states are totally hypocritical when it comes to terrorism. For instance, when the King David hotel in Jerusalem was blown up in 1946 killing 91 people and injuring 45, most of them civilians, the British state condemned the perpetrators as evil terrorists. When some of these same people formed the state of Israel they suddenly became respected politicians. You don't have to look very far to find similar examples.

"My name is Illich Ramirez Sanchez. My profession is professional revolutionary. The world is my domain." (Carlos the Jackal)

Although it is a truism that the real terrorist is the state, there have always been so called revolutionary groups prepared to use terror and the threat of terror to achieve their aims. But that is not our way.

The globalisation of paranoia post 9/11 has affected us all and the knee-jerk, cross party, consensus in the House of Commons, following the July 2005 London bombings, suits the state very nicely. If it is done quickly enough, any opposition to the implementation of the most draconian laws to curtail freedom and strengthen racist immigration policies will be seen as playing into the hands of the terrorists. As H. L. Mencken said, "The whole aim of practical politics is to keep the populace alarmed – and hence clamourous to be led to safety – by menacing it with an endless series of hobgoblins, all of them imaginary."

It is a great fear amongst activists that middle class 'revolutionaries' will be sucked into this consensus and denounce genuine attempts to change the world as they have done before (Angry Brigade et al). As here in the UK policy changes between news bulletins, there is no point detailing the possible consequences of even planning an action. What is certain however is that, without some kind of popular backlash, the powers of the secret state will continue to be augmented all the time. And to justify their existence the spooks will be using their new powers against us.

As I write this, Tony Blair's self-awarded carte blanche appears to be under threat as 'rebels' in his own party helped defeat measures allowing detention without charge of terrorist suspects for up to 90 days. The fall back position however doubles the current detention period to 28 days – hooray. This vote, seen as a huge blow to Blair, is obviously not a reversal, merely a change of gear as the anti-terror juggernaut carries us inexorably toward the perfect police state.

COME FLY WITH ME

Meanwhile our American chums (with the complicity, they allege, of European governments) have been indulging in a bit of package tour torture with the CIA acting as travel agent. They have been shipping people between secret prisons in Europe and then 'rendering' (another conflict, another obscenity) them on to be tortured. The globalisation of the police state.

PART TWO

PREPARING FOR THE PARTY

"A man with deep far-sightedness will survey both the beginning and the end of a situation and continually consider its every facet as important." (Takeda Shingen, 1521-1573)

Part Two covers researching the target, planning and all the little details that should be considered.

PRE-PLANNING
Before embarking upon the planning phase proper you should know what you are up against generally. Knowledge could be freedom in a very real sense.

Forensics
Even before the planning phase it is vital that forensics are considered. As it is such an important consideration I make no apologies for giving it such a large section and going into quite a lot of detail in Appendix iii. It is important that you understand the basics of forensics and that you work out ways to minimise the amount of evidence you leave at the scene and bring home from the scene. It may be years later that the DNA evidence obtained from a drop of blood that came from a cut you sustained while breaking into a building comes back to haunt you.

HAS ANYONE SEEN MY FOLLICLE?
Every action leaves some form of imprint on the world. We leave evidence of our presence everywhere we go and we carry with us evidence of everywhere we have been and everyone we have been in contact with. This is known as Locard's Exchange Principal. Your hair is constantly falling out and you leave it all over the place. Just look around your house. You pick up carpet fibres on your shoes, dirt from the ground, your skin flakes off, etc., etc. It is easy to get paranoid about the capabilities of forensic science (particularly after having done a bit of research on the subject) but we can seriously reduce the capability of the cops to use forensics against us by taking a few precautions. Here, in brief, are some of the techniques that could be used against us.

TOOL MARK IDENTIFICATION
Most physical evidence concerns itself with class characteristics and individual characteristics. Class characteristics are those characteristics which are common to a group of similar objects. Individual characteristics are those characteristics which are unique to a given object and set it apart from similar objects. These two concepts, class and individual characteristics are the most important in tool mark

examination. With shoes and boots it is possible to cover the soles with home made overshoes which you will dump after the action.

IMPRINT EVIDENCE
There are two basic types of imprint evidence: **three dimensional** impressions, in which an object presses into something soft which retains the impression of that object (your footprints in mud would be an example); and **two dimensional** impressions, in which an object transfers an image to a surface or an object comes into contact with a surface that is coated and removes some of that coating, scraping the paint off your vehicle perhaps.

Impression evidence can be so detailed, to the microscopic level, that it can be used to identify both class and individual characteristics. Not just used for shoes, impression evidence can also be used with tire impressions (a tire impression is just like a long, continuous shoe impression) and tool marks.

TOOLMARK EVIDENCE

There are three types of tool mark impressions: **compression**, in which a tool surface presses into a softer material; **sliding**, in which a tool, such as a screwdriver, scrapes across a surface causing parallel striations; and **cutting**, which is a combination of the above two types (as with scissors). All three types can yield class and individual characteristics. In this way, marks left on a doorway from a crowbar can be matched back to that specific crowbar. This is a good reason for hiring equipment or disposing of tools after each action, which is an expensive option.

EXPLOSIVES
Without getting too into it, explosives residue can be analysed to determine the type of explosive used in a particular detonation. Also, some manufacturers are now putting chemical tags in their explosives that will allow for tracking of specific batches by chemical composition or other tags.

HANDWRITING ANALYSIS
Handwriting analysis involves painstaking examination of the design, shape and structure of handwriting to determine authorship of a given handwriting sample. The basic principle underlying handwriting analysis is that no two people write the exact same thing the exact same way. Ensure that you do not leave a hand written trail to your door. Get someone not involved in the action to sign hire documents for tools, etc.

PHOTOCOPIERS AND LASER PRINTERS

There are many ways to match a page back to a photocopier or laser printer. Since the processes are similar, the methods used to match a page back to its origin, printer or copier, will also be similar. The paper itself can yield many clues e.g. marks from the belts, pinchers, rollers and gears that physically move the paper through a machine. Toner can have unique characteristics in its chemical composition.

FORGERY

Forgery, particularly of ID cards, is something you will probably get into at some time. There are four basic types of forgery: **traced, simulation, freehand** and **lifted**. Freehand forgeries are the easiest to detect. Simulation forgeries are easy to detect for a number of reasons. Traced forgeries and lifts are easy enough to detect, but the identity of the forger cannot be determined. It is surprising how relatively crude forgeries are not detected. This is mainly down to expectation. £50 notes, passports and credit cards are given quite detailed scrutiny, but you can get away with degree certificates and various photoshop and photocopied documents fairly easily.

COUNTERFEIT SECURITY MEASURES

There are a number of methods, both simple and complex, to deter counterfeiting of official documents but given time solutions are always found. It is very difficult for the state to stay ahead of the game. That is one of the reasons that we have little to fear from ID cards should they be introduced.

PERSONAL IDENTIFICATION:

Fingerprints

It is worth knowing about fingerprints. The more you understand the more likely it is that you will take care not to leave them. Anything left at the scene of an action deliberately or by accident or dumped subsequently absolutely must be free of fingerprints. That is all fingerprints, not just yours. If you buy something second hand for instance even though you are careful not to handle it without gloves, the person who sold it to you may have their fingerprints on record which could eventually lead the cops to you. It is probably a good idea if everything used on an action is new to you and ideally it should never be stored where you live remember Locard's Exchange Principal.

Leather gloves can leave a print that is unique to that glove and no other (leather comes from cow skin, which is just as random as human skin). Even cloth gloves, can leave a distinctive print that can be traced back to the glove that made it. Prints are left on a surface because we are constantly secreting water and body oils and other compounds through our pores. This material is left on the surface we touch in the form of a fingerprint.

Despite all these sophisticated techniques they can be defeated by always wearing gloves (very cheap garden gloves or similar that you can buy in large quantities and dispose of, or a pair of Marigolds, depending on the action) and making sure that everything you carry that is to be dumped, may have to be abandoned or could be inadvertently dropped, has not been touched by your bare hands or has been thoroughly sanitised before going on the action. Always remember those little things like torch batteries.

FACT BOX

Gloves don't necessarily prevent you leaving fingerprints. You can actually leave prints through surgical gloves. Surgical gloves were made to keep sterile conditions during operations. They have to fit like a second skin for surgeons to be able to pick up their instruments. They fit so tightly that fingerprints 'pass through' the latex membrane. They can also be turned inside out to yield fingerprints from the inside surfaces. Leather gloves can be treated in the same manner.

DNA

According to recent news reports DNA evidence is being used in a far more systematic way as an evidential tool by the police. We are also hearing more about DNA samples from people found innocent of various crimes and youths who have not even been charged with a crime being kept illegally by police. Examining labs have samples of DNA, taken from a representative population group. These are entered into a database, to which the questioned DNA, a sample of blood or hair you left behind at the scene of the action, for instance, is compared for frequency among the population group.

Hair Comparisons

These are another biggie in forensic science. Hair can be determined to be human or animal. The body area from which a questioned hair came can be identified. Race can sometimes be determined. Disease conditions can be determined. And, of course, a hair found at an action can be matched to the person that left it there. It's a relatively simple comparison, involving side by side examination of the suspect and known hairs, similar to bullet matching.

FRACTURE MATCH

Tear a piece of paper in half. Hold the two halves together. This is called a fracture match. No two tears are exactly alike. One half of a tear can always be matched back to its other half. Remember that. If a half of something found at a crime scene can be matched to the other half of something found on you, that's good physical evidence. Bin bags are separated by a line of perforations running perpendicular to the open end. These perforations make for an easy tear and connect one bag to the next bag on the roll. Each individual perforation at the bottom of a bag is a tiny little fracture match; one half from the bag you just tore off, the other half from the next bag in sequence that is still on the roll. In this way, using the perforations as little fracture matches, a series of bin bags from the same roll can be placed in their proper sequence, as they were torn off the roll. So if the bin bag you used to dispose of evidence matches ones in your home, you are stuffed.

SAFE INSULATION
Safe insulation consists of diatoms and vermiculite. Diatoms are unicellular, microscopic sea creatures. Vermiculite is a synthetic material used in potting soil, I believe for the purpose of aeration. This is not a naturally occurring combination. Different safe manufacturers use different diatoms. These diatoms can be traced back to a manufacturer. They also have a habit of sticking to fabric (such as clothing). Unless you are blowing the safe, this will not be a problem.

PAINT
Paint can be examined and matched for colour and texture. Also, a paint chip can be fracture matched back to the point from which it originated. And, if several layers of paint have been applied over one another, a stronger match can be made. What are the chances that someone else used the exact same colours of paint in the exact same sequence?

QUIT SMOKING!
Ashes from cigars, pipes, rollups, joints and cigarettes can be differentiated. Also, butts can have saliva, lip prints, fingerprints, blood stains and bite marks. Fingerprints can even be developed from dropped matches.

SOIL
Soil can be used to associate a particular scene with a particular individual.

GLASS
Individual characteristics include fingerprints, fracture matches, saliva or lip prints (if you have pressed your face against a window), blood and prints from nose, tongue, chin or mouth.

OTHER CONSIDERATIONS: PHYSICAL EVIDENCE

Diaries, plans, manuals, stuff left at the action by accident or on purpose, communiqués, stored information on computers and paper trails from the use of bank cards and the hire or purchase of equipment. Avoid these by always paying cash and destroying or removing everything relating to the action before you go on it. Don't take anything traceable to you (like ID or engraved jewellery) on actions. Consider using false ID if you are hiring gear. If you must use a computer encrypt all files with PGP. This is available as a freeware download.

Security

To have a completely secure action is impossible. Whatever you do there is a risk of getting caught. Security is about taking measures to lessen the chances of this. So scrutinise every plan looking at how it could go wrong. Here are a few ways people get caught:

WITNESSES

That is people being able to identify you or your vehicle, not just at the action, but also on the way there, or even just leaving your house at a connected time. It includes images from CCTV or police video/stills. During the planning phase plan rendezvous, routes to the action, etc., avoiding cameras and nosy neighbours. Disguise yourselves and wear indistinguishable clothes. Don't tell people what they don't need to know.

SURVEILLANCE

This could include phone taps, post and email interception, listening devices and following you or placing tracking units in or on your vehicles. It is highly unlikely that you and your group will be under any form of sophisticated surveillance, particularly if the group is small and you keep very tight control of information. In December 2005 it emerged that George W. Bush had, post 9/11, been authorising the National Security Agency to monitor phone calls, email transactions and who knows what else, without having to go through the inconvenience of obtaining a warrant. This particular power was awarded by Bush to himself and he thought it best not to inform congress. In order to fight terrorism in the US, it seems it is nescessary to bug the phones of liberal protest groups such as Greenpeace and PETA. Despite all this, if you maintain a high level of security, keeping everything on a need to know basis and have not been infiltrated then you should have nothing to worry about. In fact letting security awareness develop into rampant paranoia is likely to be more debilitating than having your phones tapped.

In the UK surveillance may be conducted by numerous, and sometimes competing, state and private agencies including: Special Branch, the Security Service (MI5), a dedicated police task force or one or more of the numerous private security companies. The police have set up various squads to target specific groups, the most high profile being 'animal rights extremists'. Indeed the financial damage caused by animal rights groups has panicked the government into bringing in new laws aimed at these groups. Surveillance operates at various levels from the fairly routine, which shouldn't effect your activity that much, through to ones where everything you say and do is listened to and watched.

Virtually every person in the world who uses a telephone, facsimile or e-mail interacts with a system called ECHELON on a daily basis yet hardly anyone knows about its existence let alone its function. ECHELON is a computer component to a global spy system, primarily controlled and designed by the National Security Agency (NSA) in the USA, with global partners in Canada, Australia, New Zealand and here in the UK. To this day many details of ECHELON still remain a secret. ECHELON has also raised many problems as it is illegal for the USA to spy on its own citizens and the same is true for Britain, but Britain could spy on American citizens and vice-versa which is technically legal though it does give rise to ethical issues. Another issue was uncovered in September 1997 when British Telecom inadvertently released top secret documents to defence lawyers which confirmed that the three main digital optical fibre cables for Britain, each carrying 100,000 calls at any point in time, go through Menwith Hill to ease spying.

The last 25 years have seen the emergence and refinement of a new form of surveillance, no longer of the real person, but of the person's data shadow, or digital persona. Dataveillance is the systematic use of personal data systems in the investigation or monitoring of the actions or communications of one or more persons. It may be 'personal dataveillance', where a particular person has been previously identified as being of interest. Alternatively it may be 'mass dataveillance', where a group or large population is monitored, in order to detect individuals of interest, and/or to deter people from stepping out of line.

You should adopt a few common sense precautions, such as avoiding talking or communicating about anything action-related in your home, over email (unless encrypted) or on a phone. Be aware of anyone or anything suspicious particularly close to action time. This is when you should run regular checks for surveillance, which in turn will enhance your powers of observation.

Pre-Action

"Let's go to work." (Joe Cabot, *Reservoir Dogs*)

EENY, MEENY, MINY, MO
Selecting your target can be more problematic than it at first appears and depends on several factors: the experience of the group; the aims of the group; the resources of the group; the political climate; whether you are going for tactical or strategic targets (there is often confusion as to what the difference between these two terms is. I will try to give a relevant definition. Strategy is important or essential in relation to a plan of action and highly important to an intended objective. It is intended to inflict significant damage to the bad guys. Tactical operations are smaller and of less long-term significance than strategic operations. Tactical is characterised by adroitness, ingenuity, or skill); the stage you are at in any particular campaign; consequences versus rewards; coordination with other groups or parallel campaigns; whether you want publicity or not. And I am sure you can think of many more factors.

> **If you neither know yourself nor your enemy you will succumb in every battle** – Sun Tsu

So stage one should be to examine your motives for choosing a target. Take as long as it takes to do this. Don't get sucked into 'activism for the sake of activism'.

RESEARCH

Once you have chosen your target, get stuck into some serious research – find out as much as you can about the target (check out the Useful Sources section at the back of this book), use every means you can, from books/published sources and the internet to personal contacts and observation. Your investigations may throw up some unexpected information, for instance, you may find that your target has subsidiaries which are a softer option for attack.

> Before beginning a Hunt it is wise to ask someone what you are looking for before you begin looking for it – Winnie the Pooh

On the Ground

"Don't always think in a straight line." (*The Way of the Spear*)

RECONNAISSANCE

Reconnaissance (recces) are vital for producing a workable action plan. After studying all the information at your disposal, maps, aerial photography, etc., you must get on the ground to gather precise information.

There are special considerations for urban reconnaissance detailed in the next chapter.

You will need to conduct two types of recce before an action, they are:

• **General Target Recce (GTR)** This is where you confirm or disprove the information provided by your maps; suss out road layouts; circulatory systems (one way streets, gyratory systems, etc.); road sizes; traffic flow; turning places; drop off and pick up points; park up spot and alternatives; possible circular routes which can be driven during an action if park up is not possible or desirable; surveillance vehicle parking; distance from nearest police station; likely routes from police station to target; Estimated Time of Arrival (ETA) from police station to target; possible road block sites; roadworks, etc. It may be a good idea for the driver to be involved with conducting the GTR.

• **Close Target Recce (CTR)** This recce is purely to gather detailed information on the target itself.

PRIMARY CTR

If the first CTR is to be done in an urban area there should be a walk past of the target on the opposite side of the road. This will minimise detection by the targets CCTV and provides a wider field of view. A minimum of two people should perform the CTR, one walking from left to right and the other walking from right to left, neither should return. Don't divide up the CTR tasks, both people should attempt to look at everything and then argue the toss later at the debrief, where you may find you have taken in more information than you realise. If the target is not an isolated building you will need to count off the buildings from the target to the end of the block in both directions. This may be the only way to identify the target if you have to go

round to the back. The buildings could look identical or the front of the building might be painted a different colour to the back or the front might look posh and the back looks a dump, etc. Ideally those doing primary CTR should not be taking part in the action just in case they are spotted.

Planning for actions in urban areas presents unique difficulties. Maps do not show man-made features in enough detail to provide sufficient information to support tactical planning for an action. Therefore they should, where possible be supplemented with aerial photographs (www.multimap.com is a good start) and local town maps. The local council can provide large-scale city maps (they are used for planning applications, etc.), just think of a good reason to have one. The local council might also publish detailed maps on its web site.

TOP TIP

When entering or exiting the vehicle, do not slam the car doors. Instead, push on the door until it clicks. Remove bulbs from interior and boot lights so that you don't put them on inadvertently.

In rural areas one of the prime objectives of the daylight CTR should be to find a suitable area for a hide to act as an observation point (OP)

SURVEILLANCE FROM A VEHICLE

If you are going to get up close to your target, particularly in an urban environment the easiest, safest way is to use a vehicle. Care should be taken to ensure that the vehicle appears to be empty – no steamed up windows, etc. If the surveillance is likely to take a long time then the vehicle should be prepared. Insulate the vehicle to prevent noise being heard. Make sure that any lights cannot be seen from outside the vehicle. Minimise movement in the vehicle – rocking, supposedly empty, vans look suspicious. There will be more on vehicle modification later.

SURVEILLANCE FROM ADJACENT BUILDING

If surveillance from a vehicle is not possible, for whatever reason, it may be necessary to use an adjacent building, either inside or on the roof. I will leave it to your imagination as to how this should be accomplished (but see Burgling and Lock-Picking skills for some ideas). When selecting a position inside a building you should avoid lighted areas around windows. Stand in shadows when observing through windows. Select positions with covered and concealed access and egress routes.

SECONDARY CTR

If the target is in the country and the action will take place at night this CTR must be strictly covert. The daylight CTR should have found a suitable area for a hide to act as an observation point (OP) (this may have to be constructed before the CTR). The secondary CTR must be on the same day of the week and cover at least a couple of hours each side of the proposed time of the action. If the target is in an urban area and the action is at night the same rules apply but the OP will have to be a vehicle, rooftop, deserted building, etc. There will be lots more on OPs, hides and surveillance later.

On this second recce look at the target in more depth. Pay particular attention to any security systems. Actually time the different stages of the action. Think about what tools you will need to do the job and what you will do with them afterwards.

Decide what communications equipment you will need and test that it works in the area. Think about the likelihood of carrying away evidence on your clothes and look for places on the getaway route for dumping clothes and perhaps tools.

This secondary CTR should be conducted by the people doing the action.

It may be an idea to have a kind of check list in your head of all the information the CTR needs to ascertain.

TERTIARY CTR AND GTR

To be done the day before or same day as the action to check for physical changes to target or surrounding area.

PRIMARY PLAN

After the first recce sit down with the rest of the people taking part in the action in a secure location and work out a basic plan. This should include a route to the target that is free of CCTV. Identify a drop off or park up point, entrance point(s) into the target, exit point(s) and escape route(s).

It should be decided when the action will take place, what time of day or night, roughly how long each part will take (getting to the drop off point, drop off point to target, doing the action, re-grouping, getting back to the pick up point and getting away) and how many people will be needed. The plan should include where the vehicle will be left/taken and possible routes there.

The plan should also involve communications. This includes who might need to communicate, with whom and how on the

FACT BOX

The UK is the largest user of CCTV on the planet. Many CCTV cameras are connected to numberplate recognition technology. London has recently installed 800 extra congestion charge cameras. The average person on foot is filmed every five minutes. Smart CCTV combined with facial recognition software can check a million faceprints per second.

action. This might be between drivers and the people they have dropped off, lookouts and people on the action or a radio scanner monitor and everybody else.

DETAILED ACTION PLAN

"When you are a Bear of Very Little Brain, and Think of Things, you find sometimes that a Thing which seemed very Thingish inside you is quite different when it gets out into the open and has other people looking at it." (Winnie the Pooh)

ANALYSIS

When you have gathered all the information you can, it is time to put it to use. You should now know the disposition of security and their routines, access and egress routes, perimeter defences, positions of surveillance cameras, alarms, etc. You should also know which way doors, gates and windows open and if they open fully or are restricted in some way and whether they squeak or not. Try to determine types of locks thickness, of wire, etc. You should have at least a rough idea of dimensions. This information must now be analysed in preparation for the next step.

MODELLING

A detailed study of the target needs to take place. First large sketches can be used but to get a real understanding, a scale 3D model of the target location needs to be made. This is where the nerds who managed to stay awake during Blue Peter will come in handy. They can direct the rest of you in the uses of sticky back plastic, egg cartons and toilet rolls. The model certainly does not have to be perfect, as long as it is of about the right scale and has all the relevant bits, it will be fine. The model will give people a much better idea of their role on the ground. In the unlikely event of being able to practice the action at 1:1 scale you should go for it. You might want to paint the model with the target zone (see below) colours to help those members of the group who have visual memories.

TARGET ZONES

Concise communications are important during an action, so when it comes to discussing the target building different parts of the building should be designated by colours, numbers and letters like this: Aspects of building. Front of building – white; Back – black; Right – red; Left – green. Floors: Ground floor – one, then two, three, etc., as you go up. Windows: (from left to right) A, B, C, etc. Use phonetic alphabet (see Appendix i) to be clear when you are using radios. Doors: door one, door two, etc. So if you want to indicate the third window from the left on the first floor at the front of the building you would say: "White – two – Charlie".

After gathering all this information, it should be collated and an action plan drawn up by one person. The plan should be brought before the group who will then try to pick holes in it and formulate scenarios to deal with every eventuality (Actions On, see below). This plan should fill out the basic plan with all the rest of the information needed to carry out the action. It should go from the point people meet to go on the action to the point people disperse at the end. It needs to include precise timings, which routes will be taken, what will be happening at each stage of the action, who will be communicating with whom, what tools and other equipment will be needed, what will happen to the vehicle, and what roles need to be filled, e.g. driver, navigator, spotters, etc.

> Pooh looked at his two hands. He knew that one of them was the right, and he knew that when you had decided which one of them was the right, then the other was the left, but he never could remember how to begin – Winnie the Pooh

ACTIONS ON

If you have ever done a risk assessment you will immediately understand the concept of 'actions on'. Basically you need to imagine every possible scenario that will land you in the shit, from vehicle problems to the cops arriving on the scene. The scenarios must be detailed – the cops arrive from your front/back/left/right/several directions at once – numbers of cops are one/two/mob-handed – armed with truncheons/CS/guns. Detail your options – escape routes/fighting. How can you avoid all this happening, surveillance/communications, etc., etc. These must be gone over again and again so that everyone knows what to do in any eventuality.

The plan should also identify places to dump incriminating evidence. You should avoid dumping clothes, tools, etc. on the getaway route – they may contain valuable DNA, fingerprint or other evidence. (See section on Forensics.) Sure, dispose of them before you get home, if you want, but make a detour to do so and make sure that the people most likely to discover them will not connect them to your 'crime' and contact the cops.

If it becomes necessary to use written notes and maps in preparing for an action, destroy all such paperwork before commencing work. The best way to destroy paperwork is by burning. Since intact ashes can be analyzed in the laboratory to reveal something of their contents, even ashes should be crushed and disposed of. Outdoors, grind up the ashes and bury them. Indoors, flush them down the toilet.

Rendezvous (RVs) and Emergency Rendezvous (ERVs)

Spend time and care on selecting your RV as this phase of the action is potentially the most hazardous and the time when the group could get busted en masse. I will be describing several types of RV. You will have to decide which is the most suitable for each particular action. You will probably, with a detailed knowledge of a particular area, be able to come up with many variations.

SETTING RVS AND ERVS:

RVS

Depending on the distance from the target the obvious RV will be a vehicle/bus/train station so you can leave the area immediately after meeting up. If the RV is somewhere else make sure that you can find it, that you can approach tactically, i.e. see without being seen, and that you can tell quickly if it has been compromised, e.g. cops swarming all over the vehicle – other members busted – or you may see that the RV is being watched or you might have that gut feeling that something is wrong.

Hanging about an RV is not a good idea so only have it open at specific times, e.g. have the RV open at ten minutes past the hour (observers will tend to expect things to happen on the hour, quarter or half) and keep it open for, say, ten minutes. If other members are not there repeat the drill one hour later. If there is not a good reason why the other members have not made the second (or third – this will have been decided in the planning phase) RV time (other members may have lost their way for a while, had to avoid or evade police, or put in a circuitous route to the RV because of increased security or heavy police presence on the normal route to the RV), then you should head to the ERV. You should of course head directly to the ERV if the primary RV has been compromised.

APPROACHING RVS

This is one of the most sensitive and potentially dangerous phases of the whole operation with the possibility of the whole lot of you getting busted en masse. It is vital that you are certain that you are not being followed so use all your counter surveillance techniques. It is unlikely that the cops will be able to mount, at short notice, a sophisticated surveillance operation to follow you from an action or recce. So unless your operation has been compromised from the start by an informer within the group or by other means, you should be able to first spot and then throw off anyone following you. You will probably know most of the tricks anyway but there are plenty of books you can get from Amazon or Loompanics

TOP TIP
Always approach the RV tactically as it may have been compromised

which will go into details. A few basic techniques should become second nature, such as: using shop windows as mirrors to look behind you; making a 180 degree turn; going into a shop (ideally changing your appearance by adding or removing clothing, hats, glasses and then immediately leaving, etc. The whole point is to wrong foot anyone following you and make them identify themselves. To throw off any surveillance head into subways (as in tunnels under roads, but Underground stations work even better) which could well block radio communication; catch a taxi for a short distance. If you are in a vehicle go round roundabouts a couple of times, stop on the hard shoulder of a busy road or motorway.

URBAN DAYTIME RVS AND ERVS
If the RV is a vehicle, make sure that you can approach tactically and that you can tell quickly if it has been compromised. Make sure that the vehicle is pointed in the right direction to get away and that it is in a position where it will not be obstructed.

Rather than using a vehicle you may decide to use a neutral public venue. Shopping centres are great for use during the day. As an exercise, start by looking at an aerial photo of your local shopping centre on Multi Map, which now has a great feature where you can overlay a map on top of the photo. Use the various scales to get an overview of the area. Your local council website probably has very detailed (but small) maps of the town.

WHEN THE GOING GETS TOUGH, THE TOUGH GO SHOPPING
Next, visit the shopping centre website which will have floor plans. Then visit the shopping centre itself, check all the exits and entrances and where you can get to from them. Check whether the exits are obstructed or are likely to be obstructed sometimes. If they are emergency exits that could be alarmed, make sure that you check them from outside. It doesn't matter if you set off the alarm if you are doing a runner. Find an RV point that you can see from somewhere else without looking suspicious (café, etc.). That way you can get there early and watch another group member going to the RV and check that they are not being followed and that the RV is not being staked out. It is obviously very easy doing counter surveillance drills in a crowded place like a large shopping centre and you should do it on your way to the RV/ERV. If you are on the run remember to put in angles and distance. If you want to use a place like a shopping centre to get rid of surveillance that should be relatively easy under normal circumstances, but if you have done something really naughty and have the world's police after you, then you must lose your trackers quickly before all possible exits are covered. Always, always, make sure that wherever you use, it has multiple exits. You do not want to be boxed in.

URBAN NIGHT TIME RVS AND ERVS

Most of the above considerations apply for night time RVs/ERVs and evasion but the venue should be a very large and busy pub (not a club because of bouncers on door, only one exit, etc.).

RURAL DAYTIME RVS AND ERVS

See above for vehicle RV as the same conditions apply. It may be that you are a long way away from your vehicle or public transport or that there is a valid tactical decision for not having that type of RV. In that case, make sure that the RV has cover, and is not an isolated feature (single tree in an otherwise treeless area – that sort of thing) that you can approach tactically and that you can tell quickly if it has been compromised. Throw in dog legs and fish hooks as you get closer to the RV. This involves doubling back on a path parallel to your original one to see if your route is being followed. If you are being followed now is the time to disperse silently and head for the ERV.

As for RVs, make sure that the ERV has cover (this is particularly important in good visibility), and is not an isolated feature that you can approach tactically and that you can tell quickly if it has been compromised.

RURAL NIGHT TIME RVS AND ERVS

The same considerations apply but you must be doubly aware, must try to avoid using any lights and be as silent as possible. Think about dispersal – are there several ways to get away from the area?

ERVS

The ERV only operates if things have gone wrong at the RV. There is a need for super vigilance while approaching the ERV. As for RVs, have the ERV open at specific times, e.g. have the ERV open at ten minutes past the hour and keep it open for, say, ten minutes. If other members are not there, repeat the drill one hour later. If all members have not arrived within the pre-agreed number of ERV openings, then you should find your own way back home.

Vehicles

At some point in your group's development, vehicles are bound to play a vital part in the success or failure of your actions. The next bit concentrates mainly on cars and vans but many of the considerations apply equally to dirt bikes and quad bikes, which you might want to use for speed in difficult terrain, or road bikes which offer greater flexibility than cars in built-up areas. The more you rely on a vehicle the more imperative it becomes that you have at least a couple of members who can maintain and perform emergency repairs and drive to a very high standard. Do a mechanics course but also pick the brains of the instructors as to how to bodge repairs in the field. It is worth the group finding the money to pay for an advanced driving course and better still, a defensive driving course. The latter courses are often run by bodyguard training companies. In fact, if you can afford it, do an entire course and you will learn not just the usual handbrake and J-turn stuff but also counter surveillance drills.

If there is any possibility at all that you are likely to be involved in a chase then you should think about buying or better still making up loads of caltrops.

For each caltrop you will need two six inch nails. Saw off the head of the nails and grind or file it to a point. Then weld the two nails together in the middle.

Take a big hammer and whack the cross to flatten it. Then bend up the spikey ends. Chuck them out of the car window. Voila. If you have the skills and the equipment, instructions for making better caltrops can be found in *Ecodefense*. The online version can be found at http://www.omnipresence.mahost.org/ch4txt.htm.

These are commercially produced caltrops from www.defensedevices.com

If possible find someone who can teach you how to steal cars. There are times when it will be imperative that there is absolutely no chance that a car you use on an action can be traced back to you. If the 'Gone in 60 seconds' professionals are not in your immediate circle of friends then you will have to resort to the net or books. And one of those books could be *Direct Action*, which will, at the very least, give you an idea of what it is like stealing and then driving about in stolen cars.

VEHICLE KEYS

Do not carry keys with you on the action itself. Many people leave keys secreted on the vehicle itself (wheel arches, etc.). This is not a good idea as there are a limited number of places that they can be hidden. And all the places are known by car thieves and cops.

HEY MISTER POSTMAN

You should consider using dead letter boxes (DLBs). If you have read any spy novels you will know what these are. DLBs are hiding places that you can find easily, this is important when you are stressed and in a hurry. Examples might be loose bricks in a wall behind a particular tree, etc. It might be an idea having two sets of keys in two separate DLBs, say one on the left and one on the right of the vehicle as you are approaching. Make sure that you do not look obvious while retrieving the keys. Try to stay calm. Don't rush unless you have been compromised.

VEHICLE MODIFICATION:

Interior Lights

Interior lights are a total pain on an action, so just remove the bulbs. You cannot afford for them to come on when a door is opened.

There are times when you will want to be travelling without lights at night. No problem, just switch them off. That is fine except for the brake light. Now you could just rip the bulb out but it is a bit faffy and you will have to replace it before travelling in town or you are very likely to get busted. A better way to deal with the problem is to get the wiring diagram for the car and install a little toggle switch that enables you to lock out the brake lights when you don't want them to show.

Fuel

On an action you have to be prepared for anything, even doing a runner or at least taking a very circuitous route home. Both scenarios call for lots of fuel. If it is possible fit a couple of auxiliary fuel tanks, and of course always carry a few jerry cans of fuel.

There is a chapter on vehicle modification in *Ecodefense*. Get the book or read it online for other things you can do to your car.

TWO WHEELS GOOD, FOUR WHEELS BAD

'What about people powered vehicles?' I hear you cry. Good point. We will be getting into stealth and surprise lots in upcoming chapters and it is certainly not easy to be stealthy when you are driving a noisy car or a van, not to mention the environmental consequences of burning fossil fuels.

MOUNTAIN BIKES

The advantages of using a mountain bike are obvious. You can use them on most of the routes where you would be walking; they are, in themselves, a good excuse for you being in out of the way places; you will be quicker and, using panniers, you can carry some of the heavy kit comfortably (good for establishing caches). The only downside is that you can only use them until you need to make a covert approach.

As with motorised vehicles you will need to learn how to ride your bike in all conditions, navigate from the saddle and maintain and repair your bike in the field. Remember that bike tracks are as individually distinctive as footprints. If you have to abandon the bike you must know that it cannot be traced back to you. When choosing your bike try to get as much information as possible from someone who really knows what they are talking about. You want one which is light (you may have to carry it over walls and fences and across rivers), strong (carrying heavy loads travelling over rough terrain) and as simple and uncomplicated as possible (you may have to do field maintenance). If the group is going to have several bikes try to get the same model (interchangeable parts and all members will be able to maintain all bikes).

WET, WET, WET

You may not have thought of this but I'm sure that at least some of your targets would have an approach that might be accessed by water. This could be done subsurface (using wet or dry suits and snorkels dragging any kit you need in waterproof containers for a tactical approach) or surface (using a canoe).

You can of course deploy the snorkeler from a canoe. The best canoe I have found for the job is the Sevylor Tahiti Ranger. It is a very tough two-person inflatable canoe (green, of course) that you can carry, along with collapsible paddles and a foot pump, in a large rucksack.

And you could always steal a punt but that is another story.

Disguises.

Keep it simple. If possible do not wear specs on an action or recce. They can get steamed up, covered in rain and there are lots of opportunities to get them knocked off. Wear contact lenses. If contact lenses are not an option for you, make sure that you secure your specs really well. Think about reversible jackets or wear a very thin, dark coloured, windproof Pertex type top that you can take off and stuff into a pocket and be revealed in all your pastel glory.

TOP TIP

It's remarkable how appearance can be changed just by putting on specs (find a pair of specs without magnifying lenses, a pair of cheap – a couple of quid – reading specs with very low magnification lenses or nick a pair of plain glass demonstration specs from an optician) and a hat.

THE STORY

You must always have a reason for being where you are, doing what you are doing. Why are you walking up this street? Why are you looking into that particular shop window? Always have your story, it must be believable, and you should half believe it yourself. Maybe you could have a dog lead because you are looking for your dog (but do make sure you know its name, age, description, etc.). The story may have to keep changing as you change locations – be flexible but do not be without your story. Bear in mind that every time a cop stops to check any suspicious person or thing, a record is made of the event. Even if you are just briefly stopped and then released, that record may later be used to place you near the scene of an illegal activity. If stopped by a cop before you hit a target, cancel the action. If stopped after you have already carried out an action, destroy all evidence as soon as you arrive at a safe location.

ALIBI

Alibis need to be established before the action. You can work out your own alibi. As an example it could be a friend (A) making phone calls from your gaff to a friend (B) while the action is taking place. Your friend (B) would confirm you had called and you would agree on the content of the call. The police can easily check that a call was made from your house to your friend's number and at what time it was made. If you say you stayed in watching TV make sure you see a video recording of the programmes showing that night.

NOMMES DE GUERRE

Mr Pink: Why can't we choose our own names?
Joe: No, I tried it before and it didn't work! I had four guys fighting over
Mr Black! (*Reservoir Dogs*)

Nicknames are great. I have known people well, over several years and only called them by their nicknames. This is ideal. If conversations are overheard all the cops will get is a name that they can't trace. Similarly if you are betrayed it is only your nickname that is passed on.

If, as is more likely, members of the group know each other's real names then you should at least adopt nommes de guerre for the action. Don't get hung up about being Mr Pink though.

With radios always use call signs. You can utilise the phonetic alphabet generally employed by radio operators both civilian and otherwise, as in the alpha numeric formula Bravo Two Zero, etc., or you can try the Citizen Band (CB) formula – Rubber Duck, etc. So you could do 'Charlie One to Charlie Three'. Or at the start of the session you could say 'Charlie One to all call signs, radio check', and then go through all the call signs individually to check that they have reception.

TATTOOS, PIERCINGS AND INTERESTING HAIR STYLES

"The individual has always had to struggle to keep from being overwhelmed by the tribe. If you try it, you will be lonely often, and sometimes frightened. But no price is too high to pay for the privilege of owning yourself." (Friedrich Nietzsche)

It is an interesting dichotomy that while many of us would say that the prime reason for our activism is that we want to play some part in helping to increase universal freedom and individuality, we may feel that it is necessary to curb some of the expressions of our own individuality. Body art and modification can certainly be a source of both aesthetic and physical pleasure for many people. It can be seen as an external manifestation of one's individuality. It can also be a way of getting you identified by the cops. And that might be a good enough reason not to do it. For the martyrs amongst you it can be yet another thing you can claim to have

foresworn for the sake of the movement. If you are going to do it, keep it intimate. If you should get busted and the cops ask you what tattoos, etc. you have. Deny having any – it is rare that you will be strip searched unless you're caught for something really serious or they are searching for physical evidence. See Camouflage section for being the grey man or woman.

If it All Goes King Kong

Have a trusted person on the end of a phone, well away from the area the action is taking place in, who can coordinate any emergency or rescue plan. It might be helpful if they had a large detailed map of the area to direct you if you ring up and are lost. Use a secure mobile for this rather than a landline.

Members who do not take part in the action must be on stand-by to implement the 'lost comms' (a certain number of pre-determined scheduled calls have not been made) plan. This can mean lots of things. Everything could be going to plan but the form of communication could have failed. A member or members of the group might be on the run. Or, worst case scenario, one or more members have been busted. You must think of all the possible consequences resulting from each scenario and form a plan accordingly. This includes having a trusted brief. Do not leave things to chance. It is crucial that you formulate a viable plan, which, with a little tweaking, will suffice for any emergency.

INTERROGATION

If you are nicked during, or shortly after, an action you will be interrogated by a professional. If the action is not too serious you will probably be questioned by a plod; if the action is a bit heavier you could be dealing with Special Branch, MOD police, nuclear police, or the Security Service, known variously as MI5 (Military Intelligence 5) or Box. It is vital that you do not engage in a dialogue with them, no matter how innocent or conversational their questions appear to be. They really do operate a good cop, bad cop system, but of course the good cop is a complete myth. Be polite, antagonising them will make the situation slightly more unpleasant for you. Keep saying that you think it better to refuse to answer their questions until you have seen a solicitor.

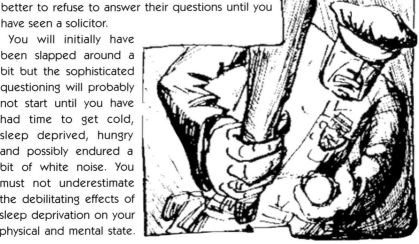

You will initially have been slapped around a bit but the sophisticated questioning will probably not start until you have had time to get cold, sleep deprived, hungry and possibly endured a bit of white noise. You must not underestimate the debilitating effects of sleep deprivation on your physical and mental state.

The interrogators will try to humiliate, scare (known as fear up) and even flatter you (ego up).

Accept any comforts offered to you graciously but not if there is a quid pro quo attached, no matter how innocuous it seems. A technique sometimes used to resist interrogation is to find a spot on the wall and focus on that to the exclusion of everything else. You can get into a meditative state and let the unpleasantness melt away. Imagine your tormentors in pink, frilly tutus.

No one can stand up to a concerted, professional attempt to make them talk indefinitely. The best you can hope for is that you can buy enough time for the rest of your group to engage in a bit of serious damage limitation.

JAIL

The British state has increasingly used jail as a form of social control and just as we are CCTV gold medallists so it is with incarceration. The Howard League released the result of its prisons survey in January 2006 and it's official – Britain jails more of its adult citizens than any other European country. It was a very close thing but we had to accept bronze for jailing our children – we were narrowly beaten by Turkey and Ukraine.

If you do get sent down use the time wisely. It can be a very worthwhile experience. You will have the time to do some of the reading, writing and research you always wanted to do and you will have the opportunity to keep fit. You will meet some amazing people and hear some incredible stories (some of them true) and you will learn a lot from your fellow inmates. Just being in prison should deepen your political consciousness and you may be able to share that raised consciousness with your fellow inmates.

Remember that you will not have been forgotten and even if it has been a mass bust you will receive support through the Anarchist Black Cross (ABC).

And finally, always remember these two famous clichés: the seven Ps (Proper Prior Planning Prevents Piss-Poor Performance) and KISS (Keep it Simple Stupid).

PART THREE

THE
PARTY

Part Three deals with the action itself and gives an overview of a way of conducting a generic action.

STAND BY, STAND BY

Before going to the meeting point for the action, run through the checklist of what you will need (see below for example kit and specialist equipment lists) and give yourself time to get it all together. Be on time to meet up so people aren't left suspiciously hanging around. It may be best to meet up at a neutral place rather than somebody's house.

Once on the way to the action, make sure everyone is clear about what they are doing. Try not to stop on the way unless you really have to, and remember that if you do have to stop most petrol stations and town centres have CCTV. All being well, you'll arrive at your destination without incident. Put any disguises, such as hoods, masks or gloves, on at the last moment, as if you get pulled by the cops it's good to look straight.

If the action is taking place at night it's best not to use torches or internal car lights for around 20 minutes before you get dropped off. This allows your eyes to become accustomed to the dark.

GO!

There are no detailed instructions for what your action should be (wrecking tips, etc.) as each action is unique. But if you want details of how to trash stuff you should read *Ecodefense* or *Road Raging*. Details in Useful Sources section at the end of the book.

LOOKOUTS

Depending on the nature of the action you may decide to place lookouts. When placing lookouts consider all possible routes of approach. Place lookouts to cover these. Once the action starts, try to keep focussed on what you are doing – but you should also be aware of where others are and what is going on around you. It's important to follow the communication structures you have decided on, e.g. making sure you are in earshot/sight of each other if you need to pass a message on/check everyone is there. (See section on signals.) Everyone should have a watch that has been synchronised beforehand, so at the designated finishing time for the action people know to RV and get ready to leave.

If there is no finish time maybe have an easily identifiable signal. Get together at the RV, check everybody is there and okay. This is easier to do if everybody has teamed up into buddy pairs before the action and then sticks together and keeps an eye on each other. If people are missing try and find out what has happened to them. Depending on the type of action and what has happened this may be the time when you want to destroy any incriminating evidence. If the action doesn't go according to plan and people are forced to scatter, try to stay with your buddy or group, move fast (but bear in mind your distance and angles) and keep in mind the direction you are going. If it's taking place at night you can very easily get disorientated and lost, so before the action have a detailed look at the map and get a clear mental map established of directions and where you could head to if this happens. The most important thing is to not panic. Remember that many people have got out of the most pear-shaped of situations by having a clear head and a grim determination not to be caught!

If it's possible get to the RV or ERV. If that's not an option get out of the area as quickly as you can, and ring the emergency mobile as soon as it is safe to do so, so people know you're okay.

Checklist for Recces/Actions

What follows is a checklist of equipment that may be needed for your recce or action. Use it as it stands or modify it for your particular group, way of working or task. Hopefully it will help avoid those awkward moments in the van when somebody asks, "So, who brought the map then?" and everybody looks blank.

GROUP KIT

• Transport with a full tank of petrol, extra cans of petrol and two sets of keys
• Vehicle breakdown and recovery details!
• Road map
• Emergency money
• Binliners for post-action evidence disposal (see Forensics section)
• First Aid kit

As well as this you will need equipment that is specific to the recce or action that you are doing. Amongst other things it may be worth taking binoculars, radio scanner, waterproof notebook and pencil sharpened at both ends, camera and Global Positioning System (GPS). The first of the European GPS satelites, Galileo, has just been launched and when the system is fully functional it promises an accuracy of one metre, which is significantly better (by a factor of 10) than the current American military system. You'll also need any tools or props specific to the tasks you are going to do on the action itself, i.e. sabotage tools, crowbar, sticks, etc. Remember to take any spares or back up gear like new batteries.

INDIVIDUAL KIT

• Spare clothes and shoes (you can rig up shoe covers so that your footprints can not be traced back to you)
• Waterproof jacket and trousers (and lightweight cover for them if they are very noisy and reflective when wet)
• Watch (make sure all alarms are switched off – rig up a cover for it – you do not want to activate a light inadvertantly, you don't want luminous dials to be seen and you don't want light reflecting off the glass)
• Masks and other disguises
• Gloves (read the forensics section)
• Small torch (best with red or blue filter and attached to clothing)
• Compass and unmarked map of the area (attached to clothing)
• Food and water (maybe a flask of hot drink)
• Emergency money (no loose change remember)
• Bag to carry stuff in
• Tobacco tin Survival kit

- Survival bag (blizzard bags are by far the best for cold weather but are very reflective – cover them with a green or black sleeping bag liner)
- Personal first aid kit
- Detailed map of action area
- Communications gear with new batteries

TECHNICAL EQUIPMENT FOR ACTIONS AND RECCES:

Cameras

To take reasonable pix get the lens size right, about 1mm per metre distance from the target. Cameras with night-vision technology can send the image to a monitor for display or to a VCR for recording. Many of the newer camcorders have night vision built right in. The original purpose of night vision was to locate enemy targets at night. It is still used extensively by the military for that purpose, as well as for navigation, surveillance and targeting. Police and security often use both thermal-imaging and image-enhancement technology, particularly for surveillance.

Binoculars

Bins are always a problem because the more powerful they are the more shake you get. The most useful bins are probably 8x30s. These are probably powerful enough for any surveillance you are likely to do. If you want something bigger you will need to stop them wobbling with a tripod or monopod. In the 8x30 figure I gave you the 8 is magnification – the higher the number the higher the magnification. The 30 is aperture size – again the higher the number the bigger the aperture, which means that more light gets in. This is ideal for low light work. There are some good Russian ex-military bins about. They are very cheap but it is worth checking them out yourself – not buying them over the net. State of the art 7x50 bins are about £300 new.

Night Vision Goggles (NVGs)

NVGs became plentiful after the end of the cold war and NVGs from the eastern European military can be bought as army surplus. There are also budget civilian models available but note that many of the so-called 'bargain' night-vision scopes use Generation-0 or Generation-1 technology, and may be disappointing if you expect the sensitivity of the devices used by professionals. Generation-2, Generation-3 and Generation-4 NVGs are typically expensive to purchase (£600 to £5,000+ for something really good), but they will last if properly cared for. Also, any NVG can benefit from the use of an IR Illuminator (which will unfortunately be seen by anyone else using NVGs) in very dark areas where there is almost no ambient light to collect. Every single image-intensifier tube is put through rigorous tests to see if it meets the requirements set forth by the military. Tubes that do are classified as MILSPEC. Tubes that fail to meet military requirements in even a single category are classified as COMSPEC. Passive NVG's are a pain to drive in. They are very heavy, give you a headache and destroy depth perception. NVGs are explained in more detail in Appendix ii.

Communications Equipment

Communication equipment should be hands free (if you have the wrong shaped ears like me, tape the ear piece to your ear, you don't want it falling out and a shouted half conversation alerting people to your presence). Work out non-verbal codes for responses e.g. press the send button once for no, twice for yes. If the channel display lights up cover it with gaffer tape. For short range comms the Motorola type two way radios are great. You can even get voice activated throat mikes for them now. Consider buying Very High Frequency (VHF) or ex-military radios for greater distance. VHF radios (which you can buy at Maplins or similar outlets) are the radios used both by enthusiasts and the emergency services and are therefore supposed to be registered and licensed. If you plan to use mobile phones be aware that they can be used to trace you using GPS technology so make sure they are secure. If you have doubts about this then buy a cheap PAYG phone – using a false name of course. Pay cash. And dispose of them after the action.

Scanners

Scanners have long been used to monitor police radio traffic and I had intended going into more detail about them. But by the time this sees print they will be a thing of the past as far as we are concerned. In the UK the police have already started to move over to an encryption system which for the foreseeable future will be impenetrable according to 'M', our electronics boffin.

The system, Tetra – Terrestrial Trunked Radio – is replacing the cops' outdated, unreliable VHF system. It gives them a mobile phone and two-way radio in the same handset, and is being implemented around the country by O2 Airwave which has a £2.9bn, 15-year contract with the Home Office to supply all 51 forces in England, Wales and Scotland through a network of around 3,500 masts. The system will be fully operational by May 2006. There are a lot of health fears surrounding Tetra mobile-phone masts. The symptoms include sleep deprivation, nausea, headaches, ear pressure, nosebleeds. They seem to stop when the Tetra exposure ends. They occur, it is claimed, because the masts transmit and receive signals on the 400 MHz frequency, which are pulsed at 17.65Hz, around the frequency at which the human brain transmits signals. It has been predicted that the occurrence of cancers resulting from Tetra could lead to "more civilian deaths in peacetime than all the terrorist organisations put together". Dr Gerard Hyland, a former head of physics at the University of Warwick, believes: "We could be seeing a pandemic of brain tumours in 10 years."

It's not all doom and gloom though. Roger Coghill, an independent research scientist and a member of the Department of Health's UK mobile telecommunications health research programme, said: "A criminal could not have come up with a better system. They couldn't have chosen a better frequency with which to disarm and debilitate the very forces that are trying to secure their arrest."

Defeating Security

This section will look at what is likely to come between you and the target and what you can do about it.

FENCES

It is quite possible that your target is protected by some type of fence. One of the most common types of fence is made of chain-link with openings of 2 inches or less to make climbing difficult. Seven feet is regarded as the minimum effective height for one of these types of fence. As a further deterrence it may be topped by barbed or razor wire. It may be possible, given the tactical situation to climb one with the aid of a ladder. If you just plan to climb it make sure you have the right footwear. You can also buy or make steps to climb these fences. They are made from a two foot strip of metal, bent in half and almost touching with four inches at each end bent at right angles to act as foot holds.

You thread them through the fence and climb. The number you need depends on the height of the fence. The top guard wire can either be cut, or covered with an old bit of carpet and climbed over. This will obviously be harder to do if the barbed wire is angled out away from the main fence. If you chose to cut it, use good bolt cutters. The newest type of barbed  tape is reinforced with a steel cable core that wire cutters cannot cut, but bolt cutters slice right through. Razor wire is the type used on government buildings but the same techniques apply. Practice all these climbing techniques somewhere first.

It is also a simple matter to cut through the fence in less than half a minute. Make sure you have the best tools for the job. Remember that, depending on how switched on the security is, any cutting, unless hidden in a low or concealed spot of a rarely patrolled fence, will reveal your presence the next morning. By cutting only at the bottom (just enough to allow you to crawl under) you can minimise this problem. Also, you can carry a few scraps of wire to tie the fence fabric back to a semblance of its former condition, perhaps delaying discovery.

Digging a hole under an electric or alarmed fence may be the only way to get through. Unless you are prepared to try and bypass the system like they do in the movies. If the entry has to remain covert remember to replace any spoil from the hole and cover your tracks.

If the fence is really isolated or where stealth is less of an issue you can, of course, just force the gates with a big enough crowbar.

If the intention is to get several members of the group inside the fence and it is not a CTR where you need to leave zero trace of your presence, then it is much faster to cut a hole than to climb in. You can use small bolt cutters or a fence tool and cut the same vertical strand of wire repeatedly each time it slants one way. You should cut the bottom tension wire also. Study how chain-link fences are constructed. Watch for electrified (see section on Crossing Barriers) or alarmed fences.

LIGHTING
The presence of security lighting often reveals the location of a sensitive target. The effectiveness of security lighting in bad weather is minimal but it could also trigger a silent alarm when activated. Time your hit accordingly. You could possibly knock out some types of light with a catapult but you would have to be a practiced shot and this won't work if the light bulbs are protected by strong covers.

CCTV
The CTR should have given details of any CCTV surveillance and any blind spots. The effectiveness of CCTV surveillance is severely limited by bad weather. Which, if this is not a 'leave no trace' job and the cameras are record rather than direct feed, means you should do the action when it is chucking it down, as all you have to worry about is recognition. That should not be a problem for us in the UK.

ALARMS
One of the most important things you will have tried to find out pre-action is what type of alarm the target has, how sophisticated it is and how it might be possible to circumvent it. Some types of alarms will be obvious from the outside and it may just be a matter of prizing the case off, removing the battery and cutting the wires. Do your homework and find out as much as possible about that type and make of alarm – the manufacturer probably publishes the specs on their web site. Some types you may not be able to detect simply by observation. Give the fence a good kick one night and hang around, out of sight and see if there is any response. If there is no CCTV in place and you are confident that you can get in and out quickly and safely without leaving any obvious trace, then go for a dry run. See if you trip any lights, bells or sirens. If it does not, there may still be a silent alarm system in place designed to summon guards or police without alerting the intruder, so hang around out of sight to see what happens. Maybe you can trigger alarms simply by throwing rocks or waving a flag. Doing this a few times (and keeping well hidden) will certainly piss off any security guards and probably lead them to conclude that the system is faulty and there is no need for them to respond to further alarms. If the action is going to be quick, alarms will be less of an issue but you should still check them out as thoroughly as is possible, particularly the response times of police/security.

Before climbing or cutting fences, check to see that they are not wired to an alarm system. Any heavy wire or conduit attached to the fence from four to five feet above the ground could indicate an alarm system designed to detect both climbing and cutting. If you look farther, you will find sensors attached at intervals.

These can be circumvented by digging under the fence, but you must be careful not to bump the fence. Another way to neutralise this type of system is to trigger numerous false alarms by shaking the fence and quickly leaving the area. Enough false alarms might bring about the shutdown of the system. Since high winds can trigger these alarms, windy nights are the best times to do this. In addition, numerous false alarms on a windy night can cause immediate shutdown, allowing you to enter later that same night.

In urban areas watch out for passive infrared motion and heat detectors. Several different types are currently in use. They can be wired to turn on lights, sound horns, or quietly notify a guard at a security station. The distance at which these devices work is limited and in many cases just flattening yourself against a wall and moving very slowly is enough to defeat them.

LOCKS

This is quite a big subject. For a start there are loads of different types of lock and, as with many of the topics I have tried to cover, this deserves a book in its own right. And of course there are books on the subject so if you want to further your studies you should get hold of one. What you are going to get here is a few top tips and a couple of, I hope, new ideas.

PADLOCKS

One of the most ubiquitous locks you are likely to come across is the humble, and not so humble, padlock. As with all the other locks, you will want to do one of three things with them: open/pick them, destroy them or prevent them from being opened. If you simply want to remove a padlock, on the older or cheaper ones you can just use a crowbar or bolt cutters. This is usually not possible with the high quality ones as they are such a good fit and there is no room to use your tools. Luckily one of those clever Greeks can come to your aid. Wasn't there something about 'if you give me a lever long enough and somewhere to stand I could move the world'. Well, you can use that ancient principle for dealing with modern padlocks. So all you have to do is to fasten an adjustable wrench (make sure it is a good quality one) or a huge pipe wrench onto the body of the padlock (you will need to put a pipe over the handle of the adjustable wrench to get enough leverage) and turn. No padlock will stand up to that. If you want to leave no trace of your passage you will have to pick it (more on lock-picking in the Burglary section later). If you want it to stay where it is the best thing to do is to squirt some of the liquid metal type glue into the keyway. You can use a syringe to squirt the glue in for that professional touch. If a syringe is difficult to get hold of then you can modify the tube nozzle or cap to produce a fine stream of glue when you squirt.

YALE LOCKS
With Yale type locks it is the same story with regard to picking and gluing. If there is a wide enough gap you can sometimes use a piece of stiff plastic (traditionally a credit card) to force open the latch. It is also possible to drill out the lock. A battery-powered electric drill with a new 1/8 inch high speed drill bit can be used to force open most Yale type locks. When a key is put into the lock it pushes up on spring-loaded pins of various lengths. When the tops of these pins are in perfect alignment with the 'shear line', the entire 'plug' in which the key is inserted can be turned and the lock opened. In most locks, all of these parts are made of brass to prevent corrosion, and its relative softness makes drilling easy. The drill is used to destroy the pins along the shear line. Be careful not to drill too deeply into the lock since this can damage the locking bar deep inside making it impossible to open. Drill in only to the depth of the keyway (3/4-inch in most locks). A 'drill stop' found with the power tools in a hardware store can be used to preset this depth and prevent drilling too deep. Inserting a pin, like a nail, will keep the damaged remains of the top pins above the shear line. Otherwise they will drop down and prevent the lock from opening. You may need to put the drill bit in a couple of times to chew up any pin fragments that might interfere with opening.

Finally, insert a narrow-bladed screwdriver into the keyway and turn it to open the lock. Before using this method in the field, buy a cheap lock or two and practice at home.

COMBINATION LOCKS
You may also encounter the combination-type padlock. To 'jam' these, pry off the dial face. Although this can be accomplished with one screwdriver, two make the job easier. First insert a narrow-bladed screwdriver behind the dial face. After it is pried up sufficiently, insert a second, heavier screwdriver to finish the job. Without a dial face, the lock owner will be unable to open the lock without forcing it.

These locks can often be opened with the same drill and bit described previously. The notch in the shackle is locked in place by a spring loaded bolt. By drilling a hole in the back of the lock case directly over the bolt, you can insert a small nail and push the bolt back out of the notch in the shackle and the lock will open.

Some expensive high security combination padlocks are designed to prevent prying the dial face off, and have two locking bolts, one on each side of the shackle. These can still be jammed by drilling a hole in the back of the casing and forcing glue inside.

Gone to the Dogs

Some of the bravest people I know are totally terrified at the prospect and then the reality of facing dogs. I can see their point. There are three types of dog you may encounter while pursuing your nefarious practices. Tracker dogs (which will be covered in the Tracking section), guard dogs and attack dogs.

GUARD DOGS

The best guard dogs are actually geese. These honkers have been protecting property in this country since the Romans were here. But you are more likely to encounter dogs so that is what I will cover here.

The function of a guard dog is to protect what it perceives to be its territory. This has usually been kindly delineated for it, by its master, in the form of a fence. These dogs can often be quite friendly but that is not the point; they will still send up one hell of a racket as soon as they smell you. I have heard that if you lie flat on the ground, dogs will see you as submissive, not a threat and not worthy of their attention – they may also piss on you just to make the point.

MORAL DILEMMAS AGAIN

As I have said before, ducking responsibility for your actions or claiming a higher moral purpose that will be justified 'in the final analysis' (whatever that is) is not acceptable – the ends do not justify the means. They are part of a continuum and if the means are wrong how can the ends be right.

I would probably not be able to take part in an action where it was intended to kill dogs unless the action really was a matter of life and death. But if attacked I do not have any qualms about defending myself and with attack dogs that does probably mean killing them. If you are attacked you will have to be totally ruthless. It really will be a case of you or them.

ATTACK DOGS

These are a different kettle of canine altogether from guard dogs. Although they might be used as guard dogs, they won't be wagging their tails, waiting to be petted, while they are barking their heads off. No. These slavering creatures just want your genitals between a couple of slices of bread – in fact, forget about the bread. These pooches can charge at 15 metres a second and weigh 45 kilos. Covering these statistics with hair, razor sharp teeth and a bad attitude makes them hard to ignore.

PLAY DEAD FIDO

You are not going to distract this lot with a Frisbee or a handful of Scooby snacks. You are going to have to take them out and I don't mean walkies.

You may be able to avoid killing the dogs in the first place by offering them drugged food (from the other side of the fence of course). But if that has not been possible and you have to get into the area the dog is guarding make sure you approach from downwind. We will discuss how tracker dogs do their job later in the chapter on tracking but suffice it to say that a dog's greatest asset is its sense of smell and the smelliest thing about you is the stink you give off when you have been sweating. This smell is heightened if you are scared. So try to be calm and approach slowly. Keep low and try to use natural ground features and use regularly used paths.

If all your stealth fails and the dog attacks, you will have to distract it long enough to disable it. You could put a stick in the way (dogs will try to paw down any obstacle between it and your rather lovely throat), or offer the dog a well-padded arm to lock onto. These diversions should give you the time to bash it on the noggin or stab it in the heart. You must make sure that it will stay down – you don't just want to make it even angrier.

Attack dogs may want to bear you to the ground before they start ripping out chunks and they will use their weight and momentum to do it. If you can break that momentum it will give you the chance to fight back. One way to do this is to stand in front of a tree and at the last minute dash behind the tree. The dog will have to check its speed and change direction giving you the opportunity to strike.

HEARTBREAKER

I have read that when German Shepherd dogs, and presumably other dogs, leap for your throat, if you can manage to stop yourself from totally freaking out, you can pull their front legs apart and that will rip their hearts in half. That would have to be a last resort.

Burglary

"Bother burgling and everything to do with it! I wish I was at home in my nice hole by the fire with the kettle just beginning to sing!" (Bilbo Baggins the Hobbit)

Part of the action, or the action itself, could be burglary. It might be an end in itself, or its objective could be to provide intelligence for a subsequent action.

There are plenty of reasons why an unannounced visit can be a good idea. For example, you may have some pesky local Nazis who have been up to no good and some up-to-date intel on their activities could be very useful. There still seem to be lots of people who insist on putting their real names and addresses on petitions, or on subscription lists for left wing publications. These things have a habit of falling into the wrong hands, as do electoral rolls. You might decide it would be nice to find out what information your nasty Nazis hold; you might also find other interesting information about them. Also burgling is just such a great buzz.

When you go a-burglaring you obviously have to decide on one of two options: whether it is going to be a covert job, looking round, taking photos, 'casing the joint' for further action or if you intend removing documents, etc., from the premises or causing a bit of mayhem.

Lock-picking is a skill which can be learnt. As with most skills there are some people who will have a natural aptitude for it; everyone else will just have to put in many hours of practice. It is very easy to get hold of professional quality lock-pick sets and lock-pick guns. I have cited a couple of good lock-picking guides in the Useful Sources section.

METHOD OF ENTRY (MOE)

There are several factors common to both options so I will describe ways of doing a covert job and you can work out the rest yourself.

Unless it is a rush job you will be using all the basics of any action, planning, surveillance, recces, etc. You may have had someone undercover who has been able to brief you on layout, location of documents or whatever, security, codes, locks, etc. If you are really lucky they might even have been able to obtain copies of keys.

UNDER COVER OF THE NIGHT

You will have decided, as a result of the recces, moon calendars, weather conditions, activity levels in the area (the best time to go in is around two or three in the morning – that is when most people are in deepest sleep, but that might be a very suspicious time to be hanging around that area), when to do the job. Do a final recce, unless there are very good reasons for not doing one. Split up to do this, as you can cover more ground quicker and have simultaneous reports on different aspects of the property. You might as well use PTT or throat mike walkie talkies – with all the other dodgy kit you will be carrying, one more item won't make any difference.

If there are enough people available, post lookouts as the burglars go in. Depending on what type of premises you are going to enter you will probably have a certain level of security to bypass. This is covered in the defeating security section above. If the security is relatively low level then motion detectors, etc., will not be calibrated to be ultra sensitive (otherwise they would keep going off all the time). With motion sensors, remember to keep your distance from them and keep flat against a solid background, moving slowly. You will have checked out the range of any CCTV coverage and how to avoid it. Keep tuned in to the environment, taking regular listening breaks, and move up to your entry point.

DOORS

If you are going in by the front door there is a chance that there is a motion activated light. These lights are there for the householder to find their key more than anything else but they can certainly make an intruder feel exposed. The sensor is activated by an object entering its sensing arc which is fan shaped. You can sometimes avoid them by approaching the door from a distance pressed against the wall. Or you could possibly crawl under the fan. If you don't have a key it is worth spending a few minutes looking around for one. Try the obvious places first: under doormats (which could be hiding a pressure plate), plant pots, bricks, etc. Then look in more devious places. It is amazing how people will leave keys in really obvious places and it will make your job much easier.

If you have no joy with the key search, then you will have to get the lock-picks out. There is absolutely no point using picks if you have not spent many hours practising with them – you'll be there until lunchtime. If they are the mortise type, check the locks to see if there is a key on the inside; if there is it means that the last person out left by another exit, or more worryingly, they are still inside. Also, push hard against the top and bottom of the door to see if it is bolted from the inside.

SNEAKY BEAKY

Now is the time to start looking for telltales. Anyone who has something to hide or protect and is switched on or paranoid will have made sure they know if someone has been visiting. A telltale can be anything: a hair across a doorway, dust, a matchstick propped against a door, anything.

The picks have done their job and the door is unlocked. Open the door slowly. It's possible that the last person out leaves by the back door (although your surveillance should have picked this up) and sets some kind of booby trap on the front door or there might be a noisy security chain in place. If everything seems ok give it a couple of seconds to see if you have triggered an alarm you didn't know about. If everything is still ok get your outdoor shoes off and change into kung fu slippers. Don't step on an internal door mat – it might be hiding a pressure plate for an alarm. In fact try not to walk on any carpeted surfaces. Alarms under stair carpets are very popular.

THE ART OF NOT BEING THERE

We all take in vast amounts of information all the time but most of it, for most people, doesn't make it to the conscious mind for scrutiny. The unconscious notices if things are out of place, even by a fraction, it notices if dust has been disturbed and a thousand other things. So it is vital that you leave the place looking exactly the way you found it. This is virtually impossible to do if you are going to do a search of a whole building or large parts of one. In the movies to ensure that the elements in one scene, cigarette ash lengths, etc., look exactly the same as in the preceding scene, polaroids are taken. This is called continuity. For your purposes this is a bit clumsy but you can take a camcorder (IR film) with you to make sure you return everything to its former position.

Just because you are out of sight in a building does not mean that you can let your guard down. Keep taking listening breaks. Remember it is possible that there is still someone inside and opening the door will have caused an ever so slight change in the internal atmospheric pressure – perhaps enough to alert a very switched on guard or a very light sleeper.

What happens next will depend on what you are after. Are you looking for a specific thing, or is this a fishing operation? If you are looking for something specific but don't know where it is likely to be then do a swift (but very careful) sweep of the building. If you do not find what you are looking for, then you will have to undertake a more thorough search.

CODES, COMBINATIONS AND PASSWORDS

It may be electronic information you are after, in which case you will probably have to fire up a computer. This can be quite noisy but it might be a risk you are prepared to take. Access to any juicy stuff on the computer will probably be password protected – but maybe not. In your research you will have found out as much about the target as you possibly can and given that people are very predictable you may be able to work out the password very easily. If it is a Nazi gaff you are looking in try typing in Adolf or Fuhrer or something. If you have exhausted

FACT BOX

Did you know that, according to the law, burglary is an activity which occurs at night while housebreaking or breaking and entering are the crimes you will be committing during the day. Penalties for the various crimes are different too and, on the sliding scale, burglary of occupied domestic premises is at the top.

names, try birthdays, etc. If they have gone for a complicated alpha numeric, regularly changing password there is a good chance it is written down somewhere accessible. Look under the mouse mat, in address books or under a pen holder. Remember to leave no traces of your activity on the computer.

Similarly if you are trying to crack a safe with a combination lock try to find out the birthday of the main user (or Adolf). You may have to try lots of permutations. If this doesn't work then go through phone numbers, car registration, etc. If they are really slack they might have kept the factory setting which is usually 100, 50, 100. The combination is most often done anti-clockwise, clockwise, anti-clockwise.

CLEAN AS A WHISTLE

When you have done what you came to do, it is time to leave and you must do this at least as carefully as you entered, otherwise you will have blown the whole thing. During the search you will have been fanatically careful with your equipment, packing away every item the moment you finish using it – you cannot afford to lose anything or leave anything behind. You will have made sure that everything is in its former place, especially any telltales you might have found. And you will slip out leaving no one the wiser except you, armed now with the wealth of information you have just gathered.

I WANNA BE YOUR BACKDOOR MAN

Entry by the backdoor often offers more opportunities for concealment. And that being the case it is often less well protected by security systems. Your surveillance sorties will have determined if the back door is the usual exit. If so it should not be bolted and it should therefore be a straightforward way to enter. As before always hunt around for a hidden key before you set to work getting in by other means.

SHE CAME IN THROUGH THE BATHROOM WINDOW

There will be no need for any lock-picking if there is an open window. Even if the window is not locked many types of older window are easily opened with a palette knife or the plastic banding used on parcels. If your nerve is up to it, upper windows are far less likely to be secured. This applies particularly to the small upper window in bathrooms. I suppose this is forgotten about because people think it is too small for a burglar to climb through, but this is never the case, unless you are a real porker. Having said that, I have still managed to rip clothing on window catches while going through these types of window. A couple of things to get right: make sure that you are not going to knock over all manner of potions and unguents (whatever they are) that seem to adorn every flat surface in bathrooms. Try to lean in and move them out of the way. Make sure that you are going to have a quiet, painless landing as it's often not possible to go in feet first. Don't put your foot in the bog or sit on the flush. Modern windows usually have security locks but (particularly kitchen windows, which are opened frequently to allow steam to escape) are seldom locked.

PAINTING THE DOOR PINK
Another way to gain entry is to just front it out and be totally obvious and therefore unremarkable. It is amazing what you can get away with if you are wearing overalls.

BLOW IT UP, BURN IT DOWN, KICK IT TILL IT BREAKS
Well not really, but I had to get one of my favourite song lyrics in somewhere. If none of the above is an option then this is where it starts to get noisy – you have also left covert entry land. The last resort, unless you are wanting to leave a message anyway, is forced entry.

DOORS
Nothing subtle to be done here as far as I know: it's either crowbar or battering ram. There are some very good high tech (if you could ever call the large lumps of metal used to pulverise a quite healthy door high tech) devices being distributed by USMC (www.usmcpro.com) that are perfect for the job.

WINDOWS
You can be a bit more subtle (and quiet) with windows. You can use glass cutters to remove a section of glass so that you can reach an internal lock, or to remove the whole pane so that you can climb in. Always remember to use suction devices to hold the glass.

If you are just going to smash the glass, you can go all Blue Peter and cover the pane with sticky back plastic (in the good old days they used treacle and brown paper). This will really cut down the noise when you initially smash the glass and it will stop all the separate little, tinkley shards from hitting the floor inside. Put your jacket over the window to further deaden the noise. It's embarrassing to have to say this but be careful not to cut yourself as you go in and out of broken windows – severed arteries are not much fun and leaving a few pints of DNA is also not a good idea. Dress accordingly.

PART FOUR

PARTY
TRICKS

1. Do not think dishonestly.
2. The Way is in training.
3. Become acquainted with every art.
4. Know the Ways of all professions.
5. Distinguish between gain and loss in worldly matters.
6. Develop intuitive judgment and understanding for everything
7. Perceive those things which cannot be seen.
8. Pay attention even to trifles.
9. Do nothing which is of no use.
   (*A Book Of Five Rings* [*Go Rin No Sho*] by Musashi Miyamoto)

Part Four covers the technical skills you will need to successfully carry out some of the more interesting actions.

This book is 'A Guide to Getting There, Doing the Business and Getting Away With It' and any group contemplating hard core actions must accept that the actions will be successful only if you have spent months (at the very least) training yourselves in various skills. The vital ones are covered in detail in the following chapters and include subjects such as Camouflage and Concealment; Navigation; Tactical Movement at night and during the day; First Aid; Survival; Escape and Evasion; Communications and other useful skills.

Everyone should have a working knowledge of all these subjects but it might also be a good idea if individuals specialised in one or more skills. For instance there could be a group medic, radio expert, etc.

One of the groups I was involved with had several of its members join the Territorial Army section of various Special Forces units. It got them very fit and they learned some of the current techniques used by the elite of the British Army. These are techniques that could be usefully employed by your group. It is also a good way of discovering what methods could be used against your group.

Navigation

"Eastward I go only by force; but westward I go free." (Henry David Thoreau)

Navigation is great and the more you learn and practice the more fascinating it becomes. (How geeky was that?) With a little hard work it should not be long before your map, which will start as a flat piece of paper, covered in largely unintelligible, coloured squiggles, metamorphoses into an easily visualised representation of the three dimensional world; the contour lines will reveal the shapes of hills, their complex topography folded into features that you recognise at a glance as ridges, gullies, cols, riverbeds. And more importantly it will show you how to tactically advance to your target – to see without being seen.

For your purposes you will be going contrary to much of the advice given in the traditional navigation books: you won't be following ridges, for example. Tactical approaches need different techniques.

These navigation notes are fairly rudimentary, as other sources of information are readily available (see Useful Sources section at the end of the book) and some kind of instruction on a course or with a proficient member of the group and huge amounts of practice are necessary. You can't acquire these skills just from a book.

NAVIGATION EQUIPMENT
For effective navigation, in addition to the appropriate maps, you should carry:
• a **compass** (see page 93) I always make sure it is attached to me – put the compass cord, which should be as thin as practicable to help with route measuring, through a zip pull. I have found the most useful compass to be the Silva Expedition 4 (most people know it as the Type 4);
• a **pen** (overhead projector pens and chinagraph pencils are useful for writing on a laminated map and it can be rubbed off after use – NB not to be used on actions), or a **pencil** (both ends sharpened) – you can use it on **waterproof paper**, which is hard to rip and you can write in the rain;
• a reliable **watch**, for timings (see SKILLS BOX) and, if it is an analogue watch, you can use it as a compass (see SKILLS BOX on page 91);
• a **torch**, especially on short winter days. A head torch is best. I use a Petzl Taktikka Plus. It is a variable setting LED torch with an integral red filter and has a massive battery life and a camouflage headband. You may need a more

TOP TIP

When navigating it is sometimes worth wearing the head torch round your neck so that you can see the shape of the skyline.

SKILLS BOX

TIMINGS are more useful than pacing over distances of more than a kilometre. On straightforward terrain an average person walks between four and five kilometres an hour. However, when you are doing a tactical approach, maybe crawling or travelling through difficult terrain or in difficult conditions, you will be travelling much slower. You should practice timings in all these circumstances.

powerful light in some situations in which case the Petzl Myo 5 (there is a tactical black version) could be the answer. You could also carry a Mini Maglight or similar pen light with various coloured lenses. It is useful getting a Nite Ize or similar headband to use in conjunction with the penlight when you need to be hands free, there are also attachments available that fit on the end of the torch and allow you to hold it between your teeth;

- a **button compass**, that you can stash away in your clothing or one that attaches to your watch – just in case you lose or break or have confiscated your main compass;

- a **pace counter** (see SKILLS BOX). I have beads on a bit of para cord that I attach to my rucksack or clothing, some people have plastic toggles on their compass lanyard others transfer pebbles from one pocket to another;

- an **altimeter/barometer**, you can now get watches with these features for less than 40 quid (try Maplins);

- something to **protect** non-waterproof maps, such as a polythene bag or map case. A technique I have used is to make a colour photocopy of the section of map I need and then laminate it. I now use Anquet map software. I select the area of map I want and print it onto waterproof paper, which is now available at outdoor shops. I get mine from Field and Trek. I usually have the area in 1:50,000 scale on one side and 1:25,000 on the other;

- **GPS** satellite navigation units can be useful. These are hand-held receivers that pick up signals from satellites circling the earth, processing the information to give a read-out as a grid reference and an altitude to an accuracy of around 10m, and soon to

SKILLS BOX

PACING can be a very accurate way of measuring distances less than one kilometre. First determine how many double steps it takes you to cover 100 metres. Count every time your right foot hits the ground. Once you are happy with measuring distance like this, find how many steps it takes to cover 100 metres on various terrains and in various conditions (deep snow, etc.). If you use the bead method to keep count you should move a bead down the para cord every time you complete 100 metres.

be 1m when the European satellites are up and running. They can be pre-programmed with a series of points along the route and will work out the bearing and distance required to reach them. However, they are not a substitute for traditional navigation and route-planning skills, which are in any case required to use GPS most effectively. Unlike compasses, GPS systems can run out of battery power, may lose satellite contact in various locations where signals are blocked, or you might simply drop it over the edge of a cliff. Oh! And remember a GPS can tell you how to get from A to B but only in a straight line. This is fine if you are on safe terrain, but if you are near the edge of a precipice with steep re-entrants or the risk of cornices you could be totally stuffed. If you are travelling in poor visibility the likelihood of a major disaster happening is of course increased.

USING MAPS

"Maps encourage boldness. They're like cryptic love letters. They make anything seem possible." (Mark Jenkins)

Interpreting a map correctly is the most basic and useful navigational skill. Maps are simply an accurate picture of the ground as seen from above, scaled down from life size and with symbols to show particular features and landmarks. On a 1:25,000 Ordinance Survey (OS) map, 1 unit of length on the map represents 25,000 units on the ground, so 1cm on the map represents 25,000cm, which is 250m or 0.25km, on the ground. On a 1:50,000 map, 1cm on the map represents 500m on the ground.

To measure the approximate distance of your route, take a piece of thin string (the compass cord will do, I have replaced my cord with very thin, strong cord for this purpose) and lay it carefully along the exact route on the map, then lay it straight along the scale line on the map's margin. With practice, you'll soon learn to estimate the distances involved by eye. As an extra guide, OS maps are divided into grid squares that represent a square kilometre on the ground (about 1.5km corner to corner). But don't forget the extra effort of climbing hills when estimating how long the route will take to walk (see Naismith's Rule).

To find out which features the different symbols represent (buildings, different kinds of church, electricity pylons, roads and railways, wood orchards, scrub or marsh and so on) consult the key shown on the map.

When one walks one is brought into touch first of all with the essential relations between one's physical powers and the character of the country; one is compelled to see it as its natives do. Then every man one meets is an individual – Aleister Crowley

Height and relief (the way the ground rises and falls) are shown on maps both by 'spot' heights (indicating the exact height at a certain point), and by contours (lines that link together points of the same height). Again, you will soon learn to interpret these through practice and experience. From the map you should recognise overall height, the steepness of slopes (for example, tightly-packed contours mean a steep slope. On very steep slopes contour lines between the index contours, which are the dark brown lines on OS maps, may be omitted altogether), and the major natural landforms such as valleys, ridges and spurs. Be careful

> **TOP TIP**
>
> Never pass up the opportunity to update your appreciation of your position. Every time you reach a feature you can positively identify on the map, you can re-evaluate your navigation strategy so that if you suddenly lose visibility, in a whiteout for instance, you are not too far from your last known position.

with contours, since the intervals between them vary on different map types. Contours also vary on the same type of map but in different areas, e.g. the interval in mountainous areas on OS maps is 10 metres but in lower lying areas, such as the Peak District or the South Downs, it is 5 metres. Harvey's maps, which are great for walkers, have an interval of 15 metres but unfortunately do not as yet have universal coverage in the UK.

Some map markings do not show on the ground, such as council boundaries (unless these follow a physical feature such as a river or ditch), contours and grid lines. Rights of way marked on maps will often be visible as a distinct path or track on the ground, but in less well-walked areas the path may not be visible.

Remember that, although a good map will remain useful for at least a few years, the landscape is ever-changing and you should not be surprised if some features on the ground do not agree with your map.

Towns are an obvious example of this but features also change in managed forests and agricultural areas (hedgerows ripped out, etc.).

HANDRAILS, TICK POINTS AND CATCHMENT FEATURES
There are various tricks you can use to get where you want to go, such as:
• Handrails, these are linear features, rivers, fences, etc. that you can follow.
• Tick points, you identify features on a map and as you pass them you tick them off in your head, this lets you know that you are on course.
• Catchment features, these are major physical features in your line of travel that will let you know when you have overshot your target.
Do not mark maps with routes, locations, target, etc., when on an action – it is evidence.

NAISMITH'S RULE

One of the ways to estimate the time a route will take is to use Naismith's Rule. This will aid you with timings (see SKILLS BOX). It allows 5km per hour with 10 minutes for every 100m climbed. This applies to a fit adult. If going down hill, you should add an extra 10 minutes for 100m descent if the ground is very steep. If it is a gentle slope you may subtract 10 minutes for 100m descended. Using Naismith it takes 12 minutes to walk 1km and 1 minute is added for every 10m climbed. This is a good estimate, and can be used along with the map to plan a route. Rest is usually added at 10 minutes rest for every hour of walking. This does not, of course, take into account the nature of the terrain, climatic conditions, tactical approaches and leisurely lunches.

You should now be able to measure a distance on the map, calculate the height gain, and work out how long the section of walk should take. This will, as with everything else, improve in accuracy with practice. In poor weather the timing can be used to calculate how far you have walked. Using this in conjunction with the compass will allow accurate navigation. Remember you should be using pacing for short distances to improve accuracy.

Here is your own cut out and keep chart:

Speed	Kilometres per hour			
Distance Travelled				
Metres	5	4	3	2

Height gain	Add on			
1000m	12 min	15 min	20 min	30 min
800m	10 min	12 min	16 min	24 min
700m	9 min	11 min	14 min	21 min
500m	6 min	7.5 min	10 min	15 min
400m	5 min	6 min	8 min	12 min
200m	2.5 min	3 min	4 min	6 min
100m	1.25 min	1.5 min	2 min	3 min

IMPROVISED NAVIGATION

During daylight hours there are several ways that you can navigate using the sun. See SKILLS BOX for one of them. Unless there is very thick cloud (quite possible in the UK) you should be able to see the general direction of the sun but of course at night there is no sun at all so you will have to use another method.

IT'S ALL IN THE STARS...

In the northern hemisphere we can use the North Star which is sometimes called the Polar Star or Polaris. The North Star is always less than 1° off true north and does not move because the axis of the earth is pointed toward it. The North Star is part of the constellation called the Ursa Minor. To find it first find the Plough (Ursa Major) – it looks like a frying pan – and Cassiopeia, which has five stars that form a shape like a 'W' on its side. To avoid confusion you should use the Plough and Cassiopeia together. They are always directly opposite each other and rotate counter clockwise around Polaris, with Polaris in the centre. As said, the Plough is a seven star constellation in the shape of a frying pan. The two stars forming the outer lip of this pan are the 'pointer stars' because they point to the North Star. Mentally draw a line from the outer bottom star to the outer top star of the Plough's pan. Extend this line about five times the distance between the pointer stars. You will find the North Star along this line. The North Star is straight out from Cassiopeia's centre star. After locating the North Star, locate the North Pole or true north by drawing an imaginary line directly to the earth.

...AND THE MOON

If the moon rises before the sun has set, the illuminated side will be the west. If the moon rises after midnight, the

SKILLS BOX

USING A WATCH AS A COMPASS
A watch can be used to determine the approximate true north and true south. The hour hand is pointed towards the sun. A south line can be found midway between the hour hand and 12. If on British Summer Time, the north-south line is found between the hour hand and 1. If there is any doubt as to which end of the line is north, remember that the sun is in the east before noon and in the west after noon. This is only completely accurate at the two equinoxes, but it is a really useful tool for giving a rough bearing quickly. For anyone reading this in the southern hemisphere, you should point 12 at the sun, bisect the angle between 12 and the hour hand and this will give you a line pointing north.

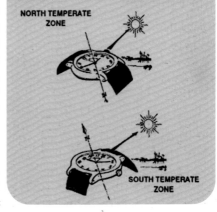

NORTH TEMPERATE ZONE

SOUTH TEMPERATE ZONE

illuminated side will be the east. You can also find south using the moon. Draw an imaginary line between the two horns and extend it to the horizon. Where it hits the horizon is roughly south. When more than half the moon is lit estimate the two points where the shadow meets the edge of the moon. These two points are joined and used as in the previous method. The most accurate method is to use a moon compass.

GRID REFERENCES

Overlaid on all OS maps is a numbered grid dividing the country into 1km squares. The numbers repeat every 100km, so blocks of 100 squares are identified by a two-letter code. By using the letters and numbers and estimating tenths within a square, it's possible to give a unique 'grid reference' to a specific point anywhere.

To give a grid reference for a certain feature (your target for example), first find the appropriate grid square. Follow the grid line to the west of your target to find its number. The number will be between 00 and 99. Let's say the number is 23. Now mentally divide the grid square into tenths – that is units of 100 metres on the ground. Count off the tenths from the 23 line to the target let's say there are four we now have 234. This number is called the Easting because you moved East. The next step is to find the line south of the target and follow it to find its number. Say 69. Now count off tenths north to the target, say 9. That gives us 699 and these are called Northings because we moved North. Put the numbers together and we have a Grid Reference of 234699.

It is easy to forget which grid line to count from first so think of a mnemonic to remember it or use the common formula of 'Along the corridor (Eastings) and up the stairs (Northings)'.

Good compasses have Romers which divide grid squares into tenths for the different scale maps you are likely to encounter. They make giving grid references a breeze. Hold the Romer zero against the target and first read the number which touches the grid line to the left of the target to give you the Eastings. Then read off the number which touches the grid line below the target to get the Northings. Fractions should be rounded downwards.

URBAN NAVIGATION

Although the principles are the same, urban navigation requires different tactics to rural/mountainous navigation. You should write down or memorise the route through an urban area as a step-by-step process. For example, 'Go three blocks north, turn left (west) on a wide divided road until you go over a river bridge. Turn right (north) along the west bank of the river, and…'

While studying the map (an A to Z rather than an OS now, of course) and operating in a built-up area, work hard to develop an understanding (mental map) of the entire area. This advantage will allow you to navigate over multiple routes to any location. It will also preclude your getting lost whenever you miss a turn or are forced off the planned route by obstacles or the tactical situation (daylight hours, police presence, etc.).

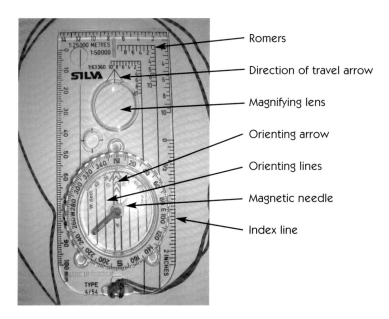

Romers

Direction of travel arrow

Magnifying lens

Orienting arrow

Orienting lines

Magnetic needle

Index line

USING A COMPASS

In lowland areas you could rely purely on map-reading skills, but using map and compass together, provided you have the basic skills, will help you follow your route with much more accuracy, particularly in woods. In the hills a compass is essential, especially when visibility is poor. Choose an orienteering or protractor compass with a rectangular base plate of reasonable size so it can be turned while wearing gloves, and clearly marked km/m scales that can be read in poor light.

SET THE MAP

Use the compass to ensure that the map is aligned in the direction you are facing so that the features on the map match those on the ground.

TAKING A BEARING

A bearing is the angle between north and the direction you want to go. You should first measure

TOP TIP

It is easy to forget whether you are supposed to add or subtract declination and there are many formulas for remembering, or you can create your own. Mine is 'Grid to mag, add; mag to grid, get rid'.

SKILLS BOX

RESECTION

Use the direction of travel arrow to aim the compass at the first known feature. Make sure you keep the compass horizontal to allow the compass needle to move freely. Rotate the compass housing, while keeping the direction of travel arrow on target, so that the north end of the needle lies within the compass orienting arrow. The bearing you can now read off under the index line is the magnetic bearing to the feature. The next step is to subtract the declination. Place the compass on the map with the direction of travel end of the base plate edge on the feature. Move the compass until the orienting lines are parallel with the grid lines on the map. Using the edge of the compass, draw a line on the map. You are somewhere on this line. Repeat this process, if possible, twice more and you will have created a cocked hat triangle. Your position is within this triangle.

the bearing from 'grid north' on the map to your objective. Then, for accuracy you will have to convert this to a bearing from 'magnetic north', which is about three degrees west of grid north in the UK in 2006 but is moving eastwards. The variation or declination is given in the map marginalia. Finally, you align your compass with the ground and travel along the correct bearing. The way to get from point A to point B is to lay the compass on the map so that its edge is a straight line between the two. Make sure that the direction of travel arrow is pointed towards your objective.

Rotate the compass housing so that the orienting lines are in line with the north-south grid lines on the map. Make sure that the red end is pointed to the north on the map.

Add the magnetic declination.

Turn the compass so that the red end of the needle falls within the compass orienting arrow.

Now follow the direction of travel arrow to your objective.

RESECTION (SEE SKILLS BOX)

If you are temporarily misplaced – although some uncharitable souls might say you were lost – a resection is a pretty accurate way to find your position. All you need is a vantage point from where you can see two or, ideally, three known features which are shown on the map. Once you have identified your features, use your compass to plot the bearing from them back to you onto your map. Your position is where the lines intersect. If you use three points the resection will form a triangle and the theory is that you will be in the middle of the triangle. If you use two points on the map the resection will form an X, you are at the point where the two lines cross. Using three points is much more accurate than using two; the degree of accuracy of a resection should (with practice) be around a hundred metres.

ASPECT OF SLOPE (SEE SKILLS BOX)

This is a very useful technique if all else fails. It is a technique you will also use a lot in winter when many of the features shown on the map are obliterated by a covering of snow.

ATTACK POINTS (SEE SKILLS BOX)

This is a great way to find a small feature on a map, e.g. a sheepfold that you could use as an emergency shelter or for concealment, or perhaps a cache of food, equipment, etc., that you or another member of the group have marked on the map.

AIMING OFF

Yet another method for finding a precise but easy to miss location, particularly on a linear feature such as a river, is to aim to hit the river say to the left of the location you want then simply walk right. If you tried to hit the location bang on and you missed you would not know if you had missed it on the left or the right.

BACK BEARINGS

If you need to retrace your steps, particularly in bad visibility, taking a back bearing is the easiest way to do it. Don't bother to complicate the procedure by adding or subtracting 180 degrees from your compass bearing all you need to do is turn the compass so that the south end of the needle rather than north end falls within the compass orienting arrow.

TACTICAL NAVIGATION

This is where you pull all the theory together and use your navigational skills for recces or the action itself.

RIDGES

They are easy to find on the map and easy to find on the ground so they are an ideal navigational aid. Unfortunately, you can't use the crest of the ridge. Have a look at the

SKILLS BOX

ASPECT OF SLOPE
Point your compass direction of travel arrow down the fall line (the fall line is the direction in which a ball would roll) of the hill you are on; take a bearing; subtract the declination; put the compass on the map; orient the grid lines in the area you think you are and move the compass until the edge of the compass bisects the contours at 90 degrees and you are somewhere on that line.

SKILLS BOX

ATTACK POINTS
Identify an obvious feature on the map (e.g. path or wall junction) which is no more than a couple of hundred metres from the place you need to find. Navigate to this obvious point and from there you will have no trouble finding your pot of gold.

Silhouette piece in the Camouflage chapter. In good visibility use the obverse side of the ridge so you can't be seen from the direction of the target. At night it should be sufficient to drop below the skyline, enabling you to keep the target in view. Obviously don't use head torches or any other lights for that matter.

ROADS, PATHS, ETC.

Although roads and paths can be useful (easy to walk on, hard surfaces which don't hold footprints, etc.), it is a dead giveaway if you are seen on one in full camo gear during a tactical advance. And even if you hear, for instance, a car some distance before the occupants can see you it may be impossible to get off the road speedily due to the presence of hedges and fences. The same holds true for pedestrians on footpaths and horse riders on bridleways.

Barriers

Fences and walls are shown on 1:25,000 scale maps. Gates aren't however. Obviously where a path marked on the map goes through a wall there must be a gate or stile and it may, depending on circumstances, be worth taking the risk to use them. If you think this will not be an option you should do a Grey (wo)man (explained in the Camouflage section) and recce in daylight. Points to look out for might include: does the line on the map indicate a wall or a fence? If it is a fence is it electrified? Are the barriers marked on your map actually there on the ground? Some old stone walls have crumbled to such an extent that they no longer constitute a barrier to your movement. Some ancient field boundaries can be seen clearly in aerial photographs and therefore make it onto the maps but may be virtually invisible on the ground. Have new fences been erected? If so mark them accurately on your map. Check forestry plantations as their shape can change rapidly with logging clearing huge sections or new plantings blocking areas. This is very important as what appears to be cover or a barrier to movement on the map may well not exist at all. Are there crops growing in a field that will make it too time consuming to cross? Can you use the field margins? Are there noisy animals about? Is it possible to cross rivers? These are obvious considerations you will probably notice other ones on your recce.

FACT BOX

Hedgerows are being ripped out all the time by unscrupulous farmers eager to maximise their profits and uncaring for what happens to the land or the wildlife using the hedgerows. Information on missing hedgerows can take some time to make it on to the map.

CROSSING BARRIERS

Fences

There are many types of fences you are likely to encounter and you may, for tactical reasons, deal with them in a variety of ways.

Barbed Wire
If it can snag you it will. Don't rely on holding the wires apart or holding the top strand down, someone in the group is almost certain to leave skin, blood and clothing behind – evidence remember.

If you have decided that you are going to go over the top strand then take some carpet or heavy duty tarp with you.

If you decide to go under the fence, take a pair of wire cutters with you to cut the bottom strand. Make sure that both ends of the cut wire are held so that they don't go pinging all over the place. Take off any rucksacks, etc. Lay parallel to the line of the fence and roll under. It's nicer than crawling. Then pull your rucksack through. Bodge a repair with wire and pliers.

TOP TIP

To check if the wire is live, take a long piece of broad-bladed grass and touch it to the wire; gradually move it closer until, if the fence is switched on, you will feel a tingle.

Plain Wire.
Use the same technique.

Electric Fence (See Top Tip)
I just use my map case to push the wire down.

Square Wire Fences
Many of the newer fences have wire running vertically as well as horizontally to form squares. They are a hassle to cut and unless you are very close to the target it is probably best to climb over. The fence will be attached to fence posts and this will be the most stable place to climb over. Although, if minimising noise is a factor, this is probably not a good place as the wire, pulling through the staples attaching it to the post, makes a horrible squeaking sound that seems incredibly loud on a still, quiet night. Keep as close to the top of the wire as possible; remember your silhouette. Rucksacks should be passed over the fence.

Deer fences
These are a real pain in the arse. If you are not using a stile or a gate you must cut through as they are too high to climb safely. They are constructed like the previous type but are very, very high – remember a sprained or broken ankle will mean that the action will have to be aborted.

Walls
Climb them carefully; do not dislodge stones. Try to make sure that as little of you as possible protrudes above the height of the wall. Lie flat on top of the wall, then lower yourself down the other side. Pass rucksacks over.

RIVER CROSSINGS

"The fight is chaotic yet one is not subject to chaos.
When it has rained upstream, the stream's flow intensifies.
Stop fording. Wait for it to calm." (Sun Tsu)

Crossing fords and streams requires extensive group-level training. It is beyond the scope of this book to discuss water obstacles and river crossing techniques and, anyway, these techniques need to be practised with someone who knows what they are doing. Have a look at the British Mountaineering Council (BMC) website for more information on this subject. Until you have practised river crossings, only ever tackle gentle streams or cross by well established fording places (particularly at night). To cross a ford, slip silently into the water, maintain your footing, and stay alert. Begin crossing by sliding your lead foot forward and dragging your rear foot as if shuffling forward. This maintains balance and prevents being knocked over by the current. When all are across take a head count, and the group moves on. Whatever you do, don't even think of using a rope to help river crossings unless you are very well trained. Ropes are very good at drowning people.

BEING INVISIBLE.
As well as doing all this, you may have to remain undetected while approaching the target. Try to remember the six S's and an M, plus the N and the other S:
• Shape, Shadow, Shine, Silhouette, Surface, Spacing, Movement, Noise, Smell.
  Refer to the chapter on camouflage.

ROUTE PLANNING:

Length and Timing

As mentioned above an average walker with kit takes an hour for every 4-5km, plus around 30 minutes for every 300m climbed (Naismith's rule). Hills, muddy or uneven path surfaces, high winds and bad weather can also slow you down. Build in time for rests.

Meal Breaks

Look for good places to stop and eat. Keep things flexible and include extra time for changes of plan, as well as potential problems such as bad weather, tiredness or injury, and blocked paths. Recce alternative paths you find along the way. Look out for 'escape routes' and alternatives at the planning stage.

Weather

Being English, I could obsess at length on the weather, and it is a very good idea to learn the basics of weather forecasting on the hill but to go into the detail it deserves would take a whole book.

Do make sure you check the weather forecast not just on the day but in the preceding week to get a feel of the prevailing weather patterns. Get a good long term forecast that is as local as possible. You can get online forecasts on the Met Office and other sites. Metcheck is good. You must become adept at interpreting synoptic charts as that is by far the best way to get a handle on the way the weather is moving.

Route Cards

For most recces/actions you can simply memorise your route. Do not highlight it on the map if there is any chance of being stopped by the police. For training purposes a route card can be a useful resource. This should define the location of checkpoints along the way (these should be unique features such as trig points or road junctions, etc.), grid references, times between checkpoints, bearings and 'escape routes' in the event of accident, or bad weather. After training you can compare the route card you compiled from map data with what actually happened in the field.

First Aid

For this section on First Aid I am indebted to the anti-copyright information produced by the BALM Squad (Boston Area Liberation Medic Squad), with thanks to District Action Medic Network and Urgence Manif. I have made several changes and additions so any mistakes here are likely to be my own.

As this is a 'How to' manual it sounds like a bit of a cop out to say that the following notes are almost worthless without training. You must get at least one of the members of your group to go on a recognised First Aid course, get qualified and keep renewing their qualifications. Ideally the whole group should go on a course. Check out www.actionmedics.org.uk for useful information and links.

Below you will find what I hope can be used as an aide memoir to recognising and treating the most likely medical conditions you are likely to encounter on a recce or action.

THE PRIMARY SURVEY

In any first aid situation check to see if you or the casualty are in any further danger. This may mean taking a couple of seconds just to figure out what has actually happened – is your mate stuck on an electric fence with the juice still on? If so and you go to help, you will end up in the same state? Is there a danger of stuff falling on your head? etc., etc. If you have not already done so, make the situation safe and then assess the casualty. If the casualty appears unconscious check response by shouting, 'Can you hear me?' and, 'Open your eyes.' Give their shoulders a squeeze.

If there is no response and depending on the tactical situation shout for help then follow the **ABC Procedure** below:

AIRWAY

Open the airway by placing one hand on the casualty's forehead and gently tilting the head back. Check the mouth for obstructions (remove them) and then lift the chin using 2 fingers only.

BREATHING

Spend 10 seconds checking to see if the casualty is breathing. With your ear close to their mouth look down the line of their chest to see if the chest is rising and falling. Listen for breathing. Feel for breath against your cheek. If the casualty is breathing, place them in the recovery position and monitor their condition.

CHECK FOR OTHER LIFE-THREATENING CONDITIONS

If the casualty is not breathing, and the condition is due to injury, drowning, or choking, continue with sequence.

TREATMENT

UNCONSCIOUS BUT BREATHING

Place the casualty in the Recovery Position. Check circulation (including a check for severe bleeding). Treat any life-threatening conditions. Call for an ambulance. See above.

TREATMENT

CONSCIOUS AND BREATHING

Check circulation (including a check for severe bleeding). Treat any injuries. Get help if necessary.

For any other casualty who is not breathing, you are going to have to call for an ambulance, then return to casualty and begin sequence again. This might obviously be very problematic on many levels as, unless you are able to take precautions, the casualty and perhaps others may end up getting busted. This is a scenario which should have been planned for and actions on established.

GIVE TWO RESCUE BREATHS

CIRCULATION

Spend 10 seconds checking for signs of circulation: look, listen and feel for breathing, coughing, movement or any other signs of life. Current First Aid training does not advise checking for a pulse as sometimes it is too shallow to feel but I would always check for a pulse at the throat anyway, it can do no harm.

NOTE: Chest Compressions (see SKILLS BOX) must always be combined with Rescue Breaths.

TREATMENT

UNCONSCIOUS, NOT BREATHING BUT HAS CIRCULATION

If the condition is due to injury, drowning or choking:
Give 10 rescue breaths. Call for an ambulance. See above. On return to casualty follow the resuscitation sequence again, acting on your findings.

If the condition is not due to injury, drowning or choking:
Call for an ambulance. On return to casualty follow the resuscitation sequence again.

NOTE: If you suspect spinal injury, use the jaw thrust technique. Place your hands on either side of their face. With your fingertips gently lift the jaw to open the airway. Take care not to tilt the casualty's neck.

TREATMENT

UNCONSCIOUS, NOT BREATHING AND HAS NO CIRCULATION

If the condition is due to injury, drowning or choking: Give chest compressions together with Rescue Breaths (CPR) for 1 minute. Call an ambulance, then return to casualty and follow resuscitation sequence again, acting on your findings. If circulation is absent, and the condition is not due to injury, drowning or choking: Call an ambulance, then return to casualty and follow resuscitation sequence again, acting on your findings.

Continue to give chest compressions together with Rescue Breaths (CPR) until help arrives. Ensure the airway is open. Pinch nose firmly closed. Take a deep breath and seal your lips around the casualty's mouth. Blow into the mouth until the chest rises. Remove your mouth and allow the chest to fall. Repeat once more then check for circulation. If circulation is absent commence Chest Compressions (CPR). Check for circulation after every 10 breaths.
If breathing starts, place in Recovery Position.

SKILLS BOX

CHEST COMPRESSIONS

Place heel of your hand two fingers' width above the junction of the casualty's rib margin and breastbone. Place other hand on top and interlock fingers. Keeping your arms straight and your fingers off the chest, press down by 4-5cms; then release the pressure, keeping your hands in place.

Repeat the compressions 15 times, aiming at a rate of 100 per minute. Give two Rescue Breaths. Continue resuscitation, 15 compressions to two Rescue Breaths.

Only check for circulation if the casualty's colour improves. If circulation is present, stop the Chest Compressions but continue Rescue Breaths if necessary.

An unconscious casualty who is breathing but has no other life-threatening conditions should be placed in the Recovery Position. Turn casualty onto their side. Lift chin forward in open airway position and adjust hand under the cheek as necessary. Check casualty cannot roll forwards or backwards. Monitor breathing and pulse continuously. If injuries allow, turn the casualty to the other side after 30 minutes.

HYPOTHERMIA

This is a condition which occurs when core body temperature drops and is one of the main medical emergencies you are likely to face, particularly when conducting surveillance or while moving tactically to a target, as you will see from the risk factors. I have seen people with hypothermia many times and in its mild form it is very easy to combat using a few common sense procedures.

RISK FACTORS FOR HYPOTHERMIA:

Cool, cold, wet, or windy weather. Someone said 'there is no such thing as bad weather, just poor clothing'. So make sure that you have suitable clothing and equipment. Clothes that are tight and impair circulation; fatigue; dehydration; extremes of age; immobility; not eating enough; alcohol, cigarettes and caffeine are all serious risk factors. But perhaps the most serious is not taking hypothermia seriously. Be very aware and do not ignore problems.

Highest risks include days when the weather changes a lot, when it's cool but not cold, or when people don't anticipate the cold, wet, and/or wind. This is a very real danger on recces and actions where you may be static for long periods of time. You must take care to ensure that your 'clothing system' is able to protect you no matter what climatic extremes you face. It is also when using the buddy system effectively to monitor each other's condition can mean the difference between life and death. People regularly die from hypothermia in the British hills in the middle of summer.

MEDICAL CONDITIONS THAT INCREASE RISK OF HYPOTHERMIA.

Circulation problems (diabetes or other vascular diseases); endocrine problems, especially hypothyroidism (the endocrine system helps with the body's temperature regulation); hypoglycaemia; malnutrition (have less natural insulation); skin problems (can cause increased circulation to the skin which increases heat loss); head trauma (impairs the body's temperature regulation); anyone taking certain psychiatric medications. (Talk to a health care professional about these.)

TO PREVENT HYPOTHERMIA:

Dress Appropriately

Use layers, with the first layer lightweight or mid weight synthetic or merino wool (no cotton next to skin) that allow moisture to evaporate. Next, one or more thin but warm layers. Then one or more thicker warm layers (be aware that fleece soaks up tear gas and pepper spray). Finish with a windproof and waterproof outer shell or use a Pertex and Pile system such as Buffalo clothing. Wear a hat, since you can lose more than half your body's heat from your head. Wear mittens rather than gloves during static times when you do not need the manual dexterity afforded by gloves. Have extra layers available in case the weather suddenly turns colder or your clothes get wet. Wear sturdy shoes with warm socks. Avoid sweating – it makes you colder and increases fluid loss. Strip middle and outer layers as necessary to keep yourself from sweating. To prevent hypothermia it is better to be slightly cold and generating heat than excessively warm and sweating.

Eat
You need calories to generate body heat. Candied ginger can help you feel warmer if you start to get cold.

Keep Well Hydrated
Dehydration increases your risk for hypothermia. Urine output is a good measure of your level of hydration. You want lots of urine that is light or clear in colour. The risk of dehydration is the same in cold and hot weather. In hot weather people are more aware that

TREATMENT

FOR MILD HYPOTHERMIA (not moderate or severe)

• Get out of the cold and wind.
• Get warm. Move around, exercise, get your blood warm and flowing. Focus on warming the trunk, not extremities. Use chemical hand warmers, especially on your neck, chest or groin (where major blood vessels pass – with insulation to prevent burns).
• Make sure you are dry. Change out of wet clothes, especially the layer next to your skin.
• Drink lots of liquids, especially warm (not hot) drinks.
• Eat. Start with simple carbohydrates such as candy, juice and chocolate and work up to more complex foods. You should not return to the cold until your energy and fluid reserves have been replenished and you feel back to normal.

their bodies are sweating because they can see, taste and feel the sweat. In cold weather sweat is less obvious because it evaporates rapidly or is absorbed by layers of heavy clothing. In addition, simply being out in the cold causes you to pee more, losing more fluids. Finally, in cold weather people don't drink as much, because it is inconvenient or they don't feel thirsty. Many people don't get thirsty until they are already dehydrated. Consider pre-hydration. This provides a fluid 'cushion' and delays the onset of dehydration. Drink 16 oz of fluid the evening before, 16 oz. in the morning, and another 16 oz of fluid an hour before exertion. Then drink as much as possible throughout the activity (ideally 8 oz of fluid every 20 minutes during heavy activity). Don't drink liquids that contain caffeine, alcohol, or large amounts of sugar (like pop) – these may actually cause you to lose more body fluid. Also avoid very cold drinks because these can cause stomach cramps.

Don't drink alcohol. Alcohol reduces your sensation of cold and reduces your ability to deal with getting warm. There have been many cases of 'paradoxic undressing' in which an intoxicated person with hypothermia undresses and suffers from severe cold-related illness. Alcohol also increases the blood flow to your skin increasing your heat loss, and decreases your shivering response, reducing your body's heat production.

If you start to get cold take immediate action to get warmer. Don't let things progress to hypothermia. Do not sit on metal, concrete or rocks. Get out of the wind whenever you can. Always carry a bivi bag or survival shelter.

HOW TO DETECT HYPOTHERMIA

The symptoms are pretty vague, so keep aware of the weather conditions and how you feel. Consider having a buddy who you check in with every once in a while.
- **Mild Hypothermia**: Shivering – if shivering can be stopped voluntarily, it is mild hypothermia. Can't do complex motor functions with hands but can still walk and talk. Skin is cool due to vasoconstriction. Hands numb. Moderate confusion – if you cannot count backwards from 100, you may be hypothermic.
- **Moderate Hypothermia**: Shivering not under voluntary control. Loss of fine motor control – particularly in hands – can't zip up coat – due to restricted peripheral blood flow. Poor coordination. May have: Dazed consciousness. Slurred speech. Violent shivering. Irrational behaviour – may even undress. Unaware that you are cold. "I don't care" attitude. Flat emotions.
- **Severe Hypothermia**: (Don't let it get this far!): Shivering occurs in waves until shivering finally ceases. Irrational. May seem normal. Progresses to: Can't walk, curls up into foetal position to conserve heat. Muscle rigidity. Skin is pale. Pupils dilate (become big). Pulse rate decreases. Then breathing rate decreases. Then the person looks dead, but is still alive.

Treatment of moderate and severe hypothermia: Get the person out of the weather and seek medical attention immediately. Don't try exercise or vigorous re-warming. Abandon the action.

IT'S HOT! IT'S HUMID! IT'S SUNNY! (YEAH RIGHT!)

I have omitted most of the notes on heat related illness as you are less likely to have a problem with it while on an action. It is very well worth knowing but is less relevant here.

A NOTE ON REPLACING FLUIDS

If a person has been sweating, they have lost both fluids and electrolytes (chemicals in the blood, with sweat mainly salt). The problem may be even worse if they drink water without replacing salt. To correct this imbalance give water with salt, in a commercial sports drink, or water with 1 teaspoon of salt per 32 ounces of water. Do not give fluids with high sugar content (check the label – more than 5% of daily carbohydrate needs is too much) since the sugar interferes with water absorption in the intestines.

DEHYDRATION
When the body loses fluid and salt that are not replaced adequately. Symptoms include thirst, weakness, fatigue, dizziness, headache. Treat by replacing fluids and salt. Start with frequent sips as more liquid may cause vomiting.

HEAT CRAMPS
Muscle cramps, usually in the calf or abdomen, caused by loss of salt through sweating and replacement of water without salt. Prevent by replacing fluids lost with water and salt, and by getting enough calcium before exposure to heat. Treated with gentle massage, stretching, and fluid and salt replacement.

HEAT SYNCOPE, OR FAINTING
When a person diverts blood to extremities in order to get rid of heat, resulting in less blood flow to the brain. More common when someone is also dehydrated and/or standing for a long period of time. If someone who faints has hit their head or has any other problem (including stroke, abnormal heart rhythm, diabetes), treat that problem first. If the person wakes up shortly after fainting and is not confused, then they have probably fainted from the heat. Treat heat syncope the same way as mild heat exhaustion (see below). Make sure the person remains laying down for 15–30 minutes, then sits for 5 minutes. Be careful when standing for the first time, as fainting may occur again.

HEAT EXHAUSTION
Caused by loss of water and/or salt and exposure to high temperatures (although with heavy exertion this can occur at temperatures as low as 70 degrees F), leading to heavy sweating, pale clammy skin, fast heart rate, weakness, fatigue, headache, anxiety, poor coordination, vomiting and confusion. Mild heat exhaustion (someone with no confusion, vomiting or other medical problems) is treated by getting person to a cool shady place, resting with feet elevated 8–12 inches (unless there is a concern about a head injury, broken neck, leg or pelvis), loosening restrictive clothing if it is okay with the person, placing cloths with cool water or ice on the neck, chest and groin (again, with permission), fanning the person, misting with water, and replacing fluid and salt. Do not sponge with alcohol or give aspirin. If the person does not get better in one hour they should seek medical attention. Anyone with heat exhaustion should rest for at least 12 hours before further activity. Anyone with more serious symptoms, such as confusion or

vomiting, should be seen by a health care professional immediately. While waiting for formal medical attention treat the same as for mild heat exhaustion, but do not give anything by mouth to someone who is confused or unconscious. Untreated heat exhaustion can lead to heat stroke, especially in older and younger people or anyone with other medical problems.

HEAT STROKE CAN BE FATAL – AN EMERGENCY
Caused by severe dehydration and heat exposure, when the body loses the ability to control body temperature. Symptoms include hot, flushed or dry skin; confusion; shortness of breath; seizures; abnormal heart rhythms. This is a medical emergency, treated with immediate transport to a hospital. While waiting for transport, treat the same as mild heat exhaustion, but do not give anything by mouth.

BLEEDING EXTERNAL
There are lots of situations on an action where it is possible to sustain cuts (external) or have a serious fall (internal).

Aims:
• To stop the bleeding.
• To prevent shock.
• To minimise the risk of infection.

What to do:
• Expose the wound.
• Provided there is no suspected break in the bone or foreign object in the wound: apply direct pressure over wound with a sterile dressing or pad.
• Never try to remove a foreign body (e.g. glass) from a wound. Apply indirect pressure (on either side of the wound) to stop bleeding.

• Elevate part of body that's injured.
• Lay patient down to minimise risk of shock or injury due to collapse.
• If bleeding doesn't stop with direct pressure, use indirect pressure at the closest pressure point heartwards of the injury. Do not apply for more than ten minutes without easing the pressure for 20 seconds.
• Leaving the original dressing in place, bandage it securely over wound. If blood seeps through place another dressing on top.
• Seek medical attention.

BLEEDING INTERNAL
This can occur after a violent injury. If patient is in signs of shock without obvious blood loss, suspect internal bleeding.

Signs:
• Pallor
• Cold clammy skin
• A rapid weak pulse
• Pain
• Thirst
• Confusion, restlessness and irritability possibly leading to collapse or unconsciousness
• Bruising over site of injury
• Bleeding from orifices
• Unexplained swelling in one of the body's internal cavities

TREATMENT

INTERNAL BLEEDING
• Arrange urgent removal to hospital.
• Minimise shock by laying down patient and slightly raising legs.
• Loosen any constrictive clothing.

SHOCK
Remember shock can kill.

Signs:
• Weak rapid pulse
• Shallow breathing 20-30 / minute increasing to >30 / minute
• Cold clammy skin
• Thirst
• Anxiety
• Nausea
• Lethargy, confusion
• Ashen face
• Unconsciousness

TREATMENT

SHOCK
• Deal with cause if possible (bleeding, burns, etc.)
• Lie flat and elevate legs slightly.
• Loosen any constrictive clothing.
• Arrange for immediate evacuation.
• Keep warm using blankets. Do not reheat with hot water bottles or other external heat sources.

TREATMENT

CONCUSSION/COMPRESSION
Don't move the injured person (they may have spinal damage). Arrange for immediate evacuation to hospital.

CONCUSSION/COMPRESSION

These can result from head injuries. Concussion is a bruising of the brain, and compression is internal bleeding in the brain. Anyone with a blow to the head should be monitored for these. Never leave anyone with a head injury alone as they need to be constantly monitored.

Signs:
• Worsening headache
• Vomiting
• Drowsiness, confusion
• Double vision
• A dilated, unresponsive pupil on one or both sides
• Convulsions
• Signs of a base of skull fracture (raccoon eyes, bruising behind ears, straw coloured leakage from the eyes or ears)
• Deep scalp lacerations

BURNS

TREATMENT

BURNS
• Cool immediately with cold water.
• Remove any clothing over the burn unless it is stuck to the skin.
• Remove any constrictions as swelling will occur (rings, etc.)
• Extend affected area to prevent deformity due to scarring.
• Elevate affected area to reduce swelling.
• Cover loosely with clean, non-fluffy dressing or plastic bag.
• Do not use burn creams or add anything to wound.

Aims:
• To reduce heat and minimise swelling
• To minimise the risk of infection.
• Remember that the chance of infection due to burns is massively higher than through a bleeding injury.
• Be alert for shock as there is severe fluid loss with burns.

Burns are either **Superficial** (redness, swelling and tenderness), **Partial Thickness** (painful, red, raw skin and blisters) or **Full Thickness** (pale and waxy and sometimes charred skin with a loss of sensation due to nerve damage). Evacuation for medical attention is needed in either partial or full thickness burns.

FRACTURES

Treat any suspected fracture as a fracture until X-rayed.

Signs:

- Mechanism of injury and/or a history of chronic problems
- Diffuse or specific (point) pain
- Swelling and/or bruising
- Deformity
- Tenderness or point tenderness
- Sounds: snaps, pops, crepitus, which is a grinding noise or sensation within a joint
- Loss of circulation, sensation and motion (CSM)
- Wounds with or without protruding bone
- Changes in range of motion (ROM)

TREATMENT

FRACTURES

- Immobilisation with splint.
- Rest: Get pressure off the injury site.
- Ice: Cool the area for 20-30 minutes.
- Compression: Elastic wrap, e.g. tubigrip.
- Elevation: Above the patient's heart.
- Anti-inflammatory drug therapy and aggressive hydration with IV fluids.
- Allow the injury site to passively re-warm.
- Evacuation for medical attention.

STOP PRESS STOP PRESS STOP PRESS STOP PRESS STOP PRESS STOP PRESS
CPR advice seems to change almost every year – I guess they need to keep selling those first aid books. Anyway here is the very latest.
The following is an abstract from an article published in the British Medical Journal:

New international consensus on cardiopulmonary resuscitation
Guidelines recommend CPR with a compression to ventilation ratio of 30:2
The Resuscitation Council (UK) now recommends:

For adults:
• CPR with a chest compression to ventilation ratio of 30:2
• No initial ventilations before starting compressions
• When professional help is delayed for more than 4-5 minutes, one option is to give compressions for up to three minutes before attempting defibrillation
• Compressions for two minutes after defibrillation
• If coordinated rhythm is not restored by defibrillation, second and further shocks should be given only after additional cycles of chest compressions

For children:
• Solo lay rescuers should give CPR with a compression to ventilation ratio of 30:2
• Two rescuers (usually healthcare professionals) should use a ratio of 15:2

For neonates:
• will almost certainly be anoxic, so still need a ratio of 3:1

Climbing

"We cannot banish dangers, but we can banish fears. We must not demean life by standing in awe of death." (David Sarnoff)

I WANNA TAKE YOU HIGHER

Mountains are the intrusion into our plebeian realm of the very essence of the planet we all inhabit. And it is only those rendered soulless husks, who are not awed in their presence.

Climbing, in one form or another, has been used as a metaphor for freedom ever since people thought they needed a metaphor for freedom. And in the imagination one can immediately conjure up images which have lain dormant since schooldays; images from a subconscious programmed by the poetry of bourgeois, one time, revolutionaries Wordsworth and Coleridge. Their verse was inspired by and given its power during the pair's walks in the Lakeland fells.

And it is not just the English who have made literary use of upland beauty and its symbolism. What about Friedrich Nietzsche? He would have been completely stuffed if Zarathustra had nowhere to come down from.

I can think of numerous reasons why activists might want to take up climbing as it can develop lots of the skills desirable on actions, including state management (being able to change your current psychological state, e.g. feelings of doubt, fear, lack of confidence, to their opposite, or at least ameliorate them enough to let you get on with the job at hand). It can help you become more analytical (a climber, like a chess player is always looking several moves ahead, deciding what techniques to employ and where they can have a rest). Plus it is going to improve your strength, flexibility and endurance, which is nice. One of the games climbers play to improve their strength and technique is bouldering (ferociously hard climbing but close to the ground, so that the consequences of a fall are not too serious). Another game, less well known but of more relevance to activists, is buildering. With buildering the climber looks for badly pointed brickwork (or stone cladding?) etc., on buildings and then climbs them. Old railway bridges, town halls and police stations are some of the places you might want to play.

CLIMBING AND ACTIVISM

Nelson's column in London has been climbed as part of a Greenpeace stunt and must stand, so far, as the pinnacle of applied buildering. During the nineties, in the UK, climbing first began to feature in the lives of activists. Borrowing skills from the world of climbing and alpinism and indeed on certain sites having direct aid from professional climbers, activists fought the destruction of ancient woodland.

Anti-roads protesters used the knots, techniques and equipment (if not the safety aspects) of climbing to occupy and move between trees. In the climbing world, which has always seen itself as an anarchic collective and where many climbers call themselves anarchists (although we would not see most of them as such), there was massive support for the protesters and many climbers joined the actions. But in an echo of the miners' strike a decade earlier, several climbers were tempted by the lure of large sums of money offered for climbing bailiffs to evict protesters from trees. Some excellent articles, in the climbing press, were written (most notably by Jim Perrin) in condemnation of the bailiffs and in support of the activists. And in another echo of the miners' strike, long time climbing partnerships were destroyed and bitterness lingers to this day.

TECHNIQUES FOR ACTION
Out of the various climbing skills, it is tree stirruping and Prussiking that I particularly want to look at in the next few pages. They are both hybrid skills which borrow much from aspects of climbing and should be considered as valuable skills for the determined activist.

TREE STIRRUPING AND PRUSSIKING
As any roads protester knows there are many climbing techniques which can be used to imaginative effect. But these same techniques can also get you killed if you do not know how to use them properly or you become lax with your safety procedures. Or trust your life to tatty blue polypro.

Learn how to: select a suitable climbing harness, fit it safely every time, tie knots appropriate to the tasks you will be undertaking. There are many books available to help you do this but the best way is to be shown by someone who knows what they are doing. See www.animatedknots.com

SKILLS BOX

TREE STIRRUPING

Attach two of the slings to the object you want to climb using a lark's foot knot. Attach the other end of the top sling to your harness belay loop using a screw gate karabiner. The other sling you will be using as a foot loop.

Push both slings up the pole/tree as far as they will go. Next stand in the foot loop which will enable you to push the harness sling up higher. Sit back and the harness sling will cinch tight on the pole thus taking your weight off the foot loop so that you can position it as high as possible and then step up. Just continue repeating this process until you reach your objective.

Descent is achieved by reversing the process.

If you are climbing a tree and you encounter a branch which means you can't slide up the slings, this is where you use the third sling. Lark's foot it above the branch and attach it to your harness belay loop. Remove the other, now redundant, harness sling. Finally reposition the foot loop sling above the branch and away you go.

Tree Stirruping

Not unsurprisingly given its name this technique is generally used to climb trees which either have few branches you can use or the branches start high up the trunk. You might also use it to scale poles to, for instance, take out CCTV cameras or lights.

You will need: a harness, at least three slings long enough to go round the thing you want to climb, a couple of screw gate karabiners and a head for heights.

Prussiking

This is a technique that can be used for ascending or descending a rope. I'm sure you can see the applications. Climbers and tree surgeons also use variations of this technique but there is a big difference in how we would deploy the rope.

DEPLOYING THE ROPE

This is going to sound more and more like something out of a James Bond movie as we go along but curb the sniggers. If you need to get the rope over something (a tree branch, bar, etc.) these methods work well. If the object you are trying to get the rope over is not too high, simply tie a big knot in the end of the rope and chuck it over. If it is too high, tie a figure of eight knot on a bight (see picture, right) on one end of the climbing rope, then attach some very thin accessory cord (or high breaking strength fishing line but note that fishing line loves to get itself into tangles, so take care) to the eye you  have created. On the other end of the cord attach a heavy bolt or some other lump of metal – this is what you are going to throw. Chuck the bolt, this should then take the accessory cord over your object and back to the ground. Pull on the cord to bring the rope over. Now clip a karabiner into the eye you have tied in the climbing rope and clip this back into the main rope. Pull down on the main rope and this will carry the karabiner up to your branch or whatever and hold it secure. The accessory cord will now be dangling down to the ground parallel to the main rope. When you need to retrieve the rope you simply need to pull down on the accessory cord.

It's getting to be a bit more fun now, if you still couldn't reach using the previous method. The next method is almost identical but instead of throwing the accessory cord over, you attach it to a fairly heavy nut and using a powerful catapult (Black Widow or similar make) you fire it. Normally it takes an awful lot of practice to become accurate with a catapult but there is now a laser guided catapult, available at www.redsniper.co.uk, which should make life easier.

Still can't reach? We are really into James Bond territory with the next method. This technique is used by linesmen to get high tension wires between pylons – opportunities for irony or poetic justice, possibly, as there is loads of anti-pylon sabotage you can do using variations on this method, but that is for another book. This time you attach the cord to a crossbow bolt and shoot it over. This method can also be used to set up Tyrolean traverses or safety lines across rivers, etc.

The final method is to use a grappling hook or grapnel. This works very well on

buildings where you might want to get the hook onto a parapet edge or similar. The state has access to a rather nice device called a grapnel launcher which propels the grapnel with compressed air. It can also launch a flexible ladder. You, however, are just going to have to chuck it.

PRUSSIKING KNOTS AND DEVICES
Without a doubt (well, in climbing circles anyway) Carl Prussik must be one of the most famous eponymous inventors in history, second only perhaps, to Thomas Crapper. Prussik's original knot, which is now known as the classic Prussik, can rightly be claimed to be one of the inventions that changed the face of climbing and mountaineering.

These days when we talk about Prussiking we could be talking about using one of a variety of knots or mechanical devices or a combination of the two. At the risk of exposing myself as a knot nerd I am going to go through a few of the knots and mechanical devices, as they can be used in different situations.

The Classic Prussik
There are arguments for having Prussik loops of various sizes as they can be used for different jobs, but I always carry loops of the same size and modify their lengths by tying knots or adding slings. I would recommend making loops from 5mm or 6mm accessory cord. When the loops are made by tying the ends together with double fisherman's knots and leaving 3mm of tail (see left), you should be able to put the loop over the web of your thumb and have it extend to the bend of your elbow. One of the main attractions of the Classic Prussik and the reason it is still used in

crevasse rescue, is that it can be tied with one hand.

To attach it to the rope you want to climb, hold the loop by its knot, then pass the knot round the rope and back through the loop (see right). Do this two or three times more. The number of turns depends on various factors including how new and shiny the rope is, its thickness, whether it is dirty or iced up, etc. The classic bites really well, sometimes too well and to be able to slide it up the rope you may have to use your thumb on the loop that goes over the turns to release it a bit.

The Klemheist

Nowadays the Klemheist is often used as the harness Prussik i.e. the one you are relying on to stop you from falling. And it really is a great knot, being relatively easy to release after it has been under tension but very unlikely to slip. And a real bonus this, unlike other Prussiks it can be tied using a sling. To tie, pass the loop three or four times round the rope leaving a small eye at the top. Pass the rest of the loop through this eye and cinch down.

The French Prussik

Perhaps the most versatile of all the Prussiks, the French is also often known as the auto block. This Prussik moves very easily, but can release quite unexpectedly and spectacularly with possible terminal results. This is most likely to happen if the knot rubs against something. It is for this reason that for Prussiking, the French is usually consigned to serve as the foot loop knot. To tie, make three or four turns round the rope with the loop leaving equal length ends which you join with a karabiner.

MECHANICAL ASCENDERS

There are loads of mechanical devices that you can use to ascend a rope – not all of them recognised as safe by the manufacturers. Here are a few.

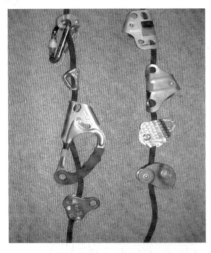

Left rope, from the top
1. Ropeman Mk. 2
2. Tibloc (best just to use this for the foot loop)
3. Handled Ascender or Jumar (you can have left or right hand versions)
4. CAMP Ascender

Right rope from top
1. Croll clone
2. Ascender without handle
3. Russian Ascender
4. Petzl Mini Traxion

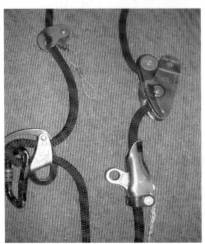

Left rope from top
1. Ropeman Mk. 1
2. Reverso

Right rope from top
1. Gri Gri
1. Shunt

And many more besides.

There are of course pros and cons to using either Prussik loops or mechanical ascenders but they often come down to weight and expense – two or three bits of string versus expensive and often heavy lumps of metal.

The Alpine Clutch or Garda Hitch, I suppose, falls outside the two categories above or is a combination of both. Using a quickdraw, clip the climbing rope through both karabiners, bring it over the top of the 'biners then clip it back through one so that the rope exits between the two crabs. This can only be used for the foot loop. The Garda Hitch is one way locking, you can take in the rope

through it but, as you stand up and put weight on it, it locks up.

HOW TO PRUSSIK

Prussiking is very similar to tree stirruping. The top Prussik is usually attached to the climbing harness and the lower one you stand in. A process of trial and error will determine what lengths of sling, or whatever, are appropriate for your size. Move the top Prussik up as far as it will go and put your weight on it. Next move up the foot Prussik. If your knee is now up somewhere near your chin that's great. If you are less flexible than that, then just do the best you can. Stand up in the foot loop and move the harness Prussik up. Repeat until you get to where you want to go. Prussik loops are not foolproof and they can release. If the foot Prussik slips it isn't a big drama but if the harness one goes you will start sliding down the rope very fast – but only for a few metres as the Prussik will then melt and you will plummet to the ground. To avoid this happening (as it's bound to spoil everyone's day) you could employ some safety measures. Some people tie big overhand or figure of eight knots periodically in the rope below them, the theory is that the Prussik will catch on the knot before it has a chance to melt. Another method, and one which I prefer, is to tie a clove hitch from the rope below me into an HMS karabiner attached to the harness belay loop. From time to

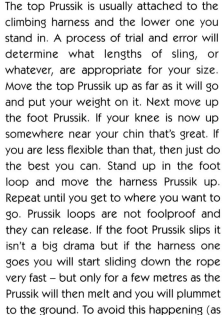

time (depending on how confident, brave or stupid you are) feed rope through the clove hitch. If the Prussik fails you will fall onto the clove hitch. It follows that the fall will be much less traumatic if there is not much rope out, i.e. you have fed rope through the clove hitch not long before.

TO DESCEND JUST REVERSE THE PROCESS

If you are ascending only, all the mechanical ascenders are much safer, quicker and easier. However, because these devices have been designed purely to ascend, coming down the rope can be quite tricky and, unless you have practiced lots, rather dangerous. There are exceptions, of course, and my favourite method is to use a Shunt for the foot loop and a Gri Gri for the harness. Look at the Petzl website for pictures of these devices. Unlike the other methods the foot loop device is above the harness device. With this set up it is simple to switch between going up and coming down.

As with tree stirruping you have to practice these techniques lots or you will be dangerously slow and totally knackered.

Fitness

"A bear, however hard he tries, grows tubby without exercise" (Pooh's Little Instruction Book)

It will, I'm sure, be apparent by now that a lot of this stuff is just not going to work unless you have a certain level of fitness. We are not talking muscle-bound gym fanatics or master race, genetically superior, über men and women but rather ordinary people developing mental and physical endurance. And that requires training. You can try all the usual stuff – running (try to run somewhere at least vaguely inspiring. If you live in the city either get out or maybe run round the local park. Vary the type of running you do to keep yourself motivated and to enhance training. Don't be too ambitious to start off with as that can do more harm than good. Aim to run for about 45 minutes at least three times a week. Try to increase the distance you can run in that time, try to incorporate hills so that you get anaerobic as well as aerobic fitness, carry a rucksack. Whatever you do try to keep it fresh), yoga, martial arts, swimming, climbing, etc., and it will certainly do you lots of good, but it is a good idea to do training that actually mirrors the type of thing you might be doing on a recce/action. The good thing about the training that is needed is that you can combine most of it.

OFF TO WALES

The SAS, an elite UK regiment, which came to the attention of the general public during the Iranian embassy siege in London in May 1980, has developed a selection process which is almost tailor made to our purposes. There are seemingly hundreds of books detailing this selection process. Highly recommended is one called *SAS: Are You Tough Enough* by Barry Davies – probably the one to get, although I haven't read it.

The gist of them all is that you can build up mental and physical fortitude and map reading skills all at the same time. The SAS, until 2006, used to train in the Brecon Beacons in south Wales, an ideal venue in many ways in that it has lots of high hills but not too high and so it is possible to go up and down lots (or one several times) in the same day. It also has crap weather and challenging map reading possibilities.

CLOTHING

As they say, 'there are no bad conditions, just bad clothing'. Well, that is partly right and, according to the mountain rescue teams, people have taken the message to heart. You are now far less likely to see people in trainers or white high heels in the mountains. After the fiasco of the Falklands/Malvinas war, where more UK troops were laid low by trench foot than by the enemy, even the British government seems to have taken the message on-board. But having the kit and knowing how to use it are two different things.

Maintaining camouflage and escaping hypothermia are not incompatible. If you are running up mountains with unfeasible heavy loads on your back, keeping warm will not be a problem so that even in winter you can strip down to your, tactically coloured, string vest. When you stop you must immediately put on warm windproof layers. Many people wrongly assume that because it is winter you always put on the maximum amount of clothing. They then do lots of hard walking and work up a sweat. When they stop, particularly if there is a strong wind, their sweat drenched clothing will suck the heat out of them and, unless they do something to combat it, they will come down with hypothermia very quickly.

My kit-monster side could easily assert itself at this moment and you would get twenty pages of geeky technical stuff about clothing, but I will restrain myself and instead give you some personal suggestions.

I will be using accepted terms for 'technical' clothing. If you do not know what these terms mean or don't understand the concept behind them, then look it up on the net where multi-gigabytes of space are devoted to the subject by people far geekier than me.

SUMMER

• **Base Layer**: Next to the skin, green, wicking T-shirt or Brynje type string vest.

- **Mid Layer**: Micro fleece (a very thin fleece with a nylon shell). The best tactical one I have come across is the Krypton smock by Montane in a rather fetching olive green.
- **Waterproof**: In summer you could get away with just your lightweight camo jacket over the micro fleece. Or you could carry ultra lightweight PacLight or similar jacket and trousers to wear under your cammies.
- **Hat**: I always carry a Buff which is a high tech version of the army headover and can be used as a hat, scarf or balaclava. It is available in camo colours.
- **Gloves**: I don't wear gloves in summer but if you have cold hands you could wear liner gloves or fingerless gloves.
- **Socks**: Some people like to wear a wicking liner sock inside their normal sock. I don't. A lightweight blend of synthetic, for durability, and merino wool or similar for comfort and the low pong factor are pretty much ideal. Carry spares.
- **Boots**: A fairly stiff-soled boot with good ankle support is needed. Synthetic Goretex lined boots are very light weight but the lining doesn't let the sweat out very readily so you end up with wet feet. I have found that they always spring a leak fairly quickly and they take a very long time to dry. So I would recommend an all leather boot. Choose one that has very few seams, as that is where water is most likely to come in. Try on boots at the end of the day when your feet are swollen and try them on with the type of socks you would normally wear. Get the boots right or you will have a miserable time of it on the hill. I use Superfeet insoles and think they are magic. Always wear gaiters if you are going across wet ground – they really do keep your feet dry.

WINTER

> "It's snowing still," said Eeyore gloomily.
> "So it is."
> "And freezing."
> "Is it?"
> "Yes," said Eeyore. "However," he said, brightening a little, "we haven't had an earthquake lately." (*Winnie the Pooh*)

All the same considerations apply for winter.
- **Base layer**: As above. Plus you might want to wear long johns.
- **Mid Layer**: I wear a Pertex and Pile (PP) shirt by Montane. It acts as base, mid and outer layer. I usually wear just a thermal T shirt for hot walking which I replace with the PP when the going slows down. If I am static I put on a fairly thin synthetic duvet jacket.
- **Waterproof**: Unnecessary with PP.

- **Goggles**: Good skiing goggles or glacier glasses are a must in the snow.
- **Hat**: I use a winter Buff or a fleece headband. You could also wear a balaclava or woolly hat. You may need to wear a helmet as well.
- **Gloves**: Mitts are warmer than gloves but they are not very dextrous. Whatever you choose carry several pairs as they are bound to get wet particularly if you are playing about in the snow.
- **Socks**: As for summer but thicker.
- **Boots**: Same considerations as summer but warmer and with a sole stiff enough to accept crampons. Make sure that crampons and boots are a good match for each other and that the sole stiffness is compatible with the crampon. You may choose to wear plastic boots. Gaiters that cover the whole boot (except the sole) are a good idea.

A lot of the kit I have mentioned is expensive and it is certainly possible to get by with army surplus kit and, with the likes of eBay, etc., it is possible to get hold of good second-hand kit – shoplifting is even cheaper.

THE PROGRAMME

An ideal training programme in the Brecons would be to start out in small groups trying to get yourselves nice and tired cross-graining, i.e. going up and down lots of hills while giving each other map reading challenges. As time goes on you should up the ante by carrying heavier loads, going faster, running down hills, covering ever increasing distances and travelling only at night. After a night exercise, start out by sleeping for a few hours after daybreak. Then progress to not sleeping at all but trying to keep vigilant. After doing all this as a team, do it as individuals; set each other tasks. Try a bit of orienteering with time penalties and evasion exercises.

THE WHITE STUFF

"Winter is nature's way of saying, 'Up yours.'" (Robert Byrne)

Now that you are feeling comfortable in the Brecons, it is time to transfer the training area to Scotland – in winter. This is a whole different ball game and the seriousness of making a mistake is magnified massively. A good area to start is the Cairngorms; the arctic plateau will challenge your navigation skills to the max. While in the Brecons you would have been using a 1:25,000 scale map for fine navigation; in the Cairngorms, in the snow, you will find that scale virtually useless. The detail portrayed on the 1:25,000 scale map will be invisible under the snow cover (so use 1:50,000) and you will have to be looking for much larger features and your compass skills will have to be spot on. Using aspect of slope to pinpoint where you are really comes into its own here. Navigating in a whiteout is certainly interesting. The disorientation is amazing and it is really easy to find yourself walking round in circles (even while following a compass bearing), until, that is, you plunge through a cornice and plummet hundreds of feet to the corrie floor. In a whiteout, which is very much like being on the inside of a ping pong ball, it can be almost impossible to tell if you are on a slope and if you are walking uphill or down. In desperation the thing to do is make a snowball and see if it rolls, which will give you some idea of angle and fall line. The weather station on the summit of Cairngorm has recorded winds in excess or 200 mph – then it broke. So it gets quite breezy up there.

Before starting the Scottish phase of your training you will have to learn a few winter skills: avalanche awareness, walking in crampons, building survival shelters and snow holes, etc., but essentially it should follow the same pattern as Wales. After the Cairngorms you could head off to northwest Scotland to experience some real wilderness.

The possibilities are huge and it can be a lot of fun. At the end of it you will have developed lots of speed, stamina and endurance. Your map reading will have improved, you will have rid yourself of any phobias you might have had about being out in the wilds, alone and at night. You will have experienced operating while in a sleep deprived state and will have become more self-reliant.

DID SOMEONE SAY GENEVA CONVENTION?

On a more controversial note, how about developing resistance to interrogation techniques? Not to mince words we are talking about torture. In the real post 9/11 world if you get caught doing anything naughty there is a very good chance that you will be tortured. After the initial roughing up, it will not be the old toothpicks under the fingernails routine – it will be psychological; running the gamut of sleep deprivation, white noise, humiliation, lies and emotional blackmail. If the cops torture you, it is certain that you will, eventually, tell them what they want to know – if the torture goes on long enough you will even confess to things you didn't do (remember the Guildford Four, Birmingham Six and numerous others?). Some people have more natural resistance to torture than others and some will succumb to one type of torture but not another. In the end the best you can hope for is that you can hold out long enough for your mates to be in the clear. It is possible to learn resistance techniques so that you will hold out longer. You could practice this stuff with your mates as the interrogators/torturers but you may not see them in the same light ever again, so you have to ask yourself if it is worth it.

Self-Defence

> "I just don't want to die without a few scars." (Chuck Palahnuik – Fight Club)

It is well worth knowing a bit of rudimentary self-defence. You never know when you will have to protect yourself from a Nazi, an over zealous cop or a left wing paper seller (thankfully thin on the ground these days). It is not easy or desirable to learn self-defence from a book. However, once you know what you are doing there are several worthwhile books on self-defence or Close Quarters Battle (CQB) which will give you plenty of new ideas. The purpose of this piece is to give you a practical overview of the subject from an activist's point of view.

THE MARTIAL ARTS
Some of you reading this probably train in one or more of the martial arts and may think you'll skip this section because you could handle most situations. This might not be the case, so stick around. While having knowledge of martial arts is a good grounding (you will have learned balance and breathing and quite likely developed your confidence), it does not mean, necessarily, that you would be any good on the street. Martial arts such as Judo, Karate, and Kick Boxing are now very much sports and have fallen victim to the stultifying rules and conventions of all sports and as such their adherents have become sportsmen and women, not street brawlers. Conventions are observed, protocols followed and rules adhered to. Participants are conditioned to respond to set moves in an orthodox way; that is why a black belt is likely to come off worst in a scrap with a football hooligan who fights dirty every Saturday.

If you choose to study a martial art make sure it is one that has lots of sparring, as one of the most useful things it can offer you is having the experience of being punched in the face repeatedly. If you can take that sort of punishment, aren't consumed with fear waiting for that first punch, continue to think rationally and can devise strategies for attack and defence, it will stand you in good stead when you learn how to fight dirty.

SPEED, AGGRESSION, SURPRISE
The cliché that says the best form of defence is attack is certainly valid when it comes to self-defence. Most of us would not normally stand a chance against someone much bigger than ourselves, someone used to street fighting, someone with a weapon or multiple attackers. Knowing a handful of self-defence techniques could give you the edge you need.

Having a few well practised moves that can be used in quite a wide variety of situations is vital but how you deploy them is the key. What you should be aiming for is to either put your attacker(s) out of the game entirely or to disable them long enough for you to leg it.

Always bear in mind the mantra 'speed, aggression, surprise'.

• **Speed**: you must move on your attacker before they can resist.

• **Aggression**: it is vital that your response succeeds, particularly if your attacker is physically superior, armed, or is not alone. So you must put everything into your move; shout, put on your really scary face, do whatever it takes.

• **Surprise**: if your response is anticipated it has already failed. It must be sudden and unexpected; this may require you to use the old magician's ploy of misdirection.

SHOUTING

"To fight and conquer in one hundred battles is not the highest skill. To subdue the enemy with no fight at all, that's the highest skill." (Sun Tzu)

As Sun Tzu recognises the sensible way to win is by not fighting at all. Talking your way out of a battering is a self-defence technique, but it has to be done with confidence and conviction otherwise you will just get an extra slap for taking the piss. You might need a good story; this should have been covered in 'actions on' during the planning phase of the action.

Do some work on your voice. This involves getting the breathing right and projecting your voice with authority. People in uniforms (cops, military, security, Nazis) are often surprisingly biddable – they are used to taking orders and it is possible for you to dominate them with your presence and the forceful timbre of your voice.

If you have worked on your voice, shouting can produce very positive results too.

STANCES

A modified martial arts stance works well (see picture, right) it keeps you balanced, solid and provides a platform from which to launch an attack.

WHERE TO STRIKE

No, not there. Yes, it can be painful, especially for a man, and there are instances where the family jewels can be a suitable place to strike (back-fisting them when you are being held from behind, kneeing them from close range or sticking a boot in while your attacker is on the ground), but generally give them a miss. The problems with going for the groin with a kick are that the testicles are not that easy to hit. For a start you usually can't see them and, unless your opponent has their legs wide apart, you are more likely to connect with their thigh. Another reason why it might be the wrong thing to do is that, unless your kick is very fast and you snap it back just as fast, they could grab your foot, which would put you in a very bad position. If you are going to kick, the best place is the knee. It is a low snappy kick that is unlikely to be caught by your opponent, and it will probably not be accompanied by a sickening, popping sound, followed by excruciating pain, which you might feel if you tried to do a head kick without having warmed up first. The knee is a great target, you can kick it from just about any angle and your opponent will go down and probably not be able to get up again.

The intention of any strike is to disable your opponent for long enough to make your next move. That might be to follow up your attack or leave the area quickly. So strikes should be to an area that will cause a devastating affect, ideally those places should be visible: eyes, throat, nose, etc., or a large enough target so that you know that you will hit it, e.g. solar plexus. You will choose which area to hit depending on several factors: opportunity, the effect you want to have on your opponent, whether you are using natural or improvised weapons.

IMPROVISED AND NATURAL WEAPONS

By natural weapons I mean your body. And there are more parts of it you can use than you might at first have thought. Here are a few bits: forehead, back of head, chin, teeth, shoulder, elbow, forearm, various aspects of the hand and fist, fingers, knee, shin, various aspects of the foot.

Unless you are well practised, a punch is likely to cause you at least as much damage as your opponent. It is safer for you to use the heel of your hand – this is particularly good for striking upwards to the nose or chin (if you miss one then you might get the other). For close in fighting use your elbows, knees and head.

Improvised weapons are all around you. You have pockets full of change you can throw at your opponent's eyes or put between your fingers like knuckle-dusters. You can jab with keys, either to the eyes or a pressure point; you can use the keys to try and slash their forehead so that they are blinded by blood. A rolled up magazine or newspaper is good and there is almost bound to be something around that you can pick up and use.

DEFENCE AGAINST WEAPONS

Almost all the advice I have read in books on defending yourself against knife attacks is crap. This is mainly because it teaches you to defend yourself against the type of attack that an attacker would not make. In the movies a knife attacker waves their blade out in front of themselves. If you think about this, it makes no sense, the knife wielder cannot thrust because they are at arms length already, to slash they would have to pull their arm back and then move forward – rubbish. An experienced knife person holds the blade down by their side, from where they can make all the stabbing and cutting moves. And if you came forward to try to control the blade you would be telegraphing your intention.

I can't go into all the techniques here but I can give you a few key points. The most important thing is to control the blade: if you try to make any fancy moves (as they do in books and films) before you have control, you will get cut. Stay out of reach until it is your decision to close the gap. Do any blocks with the outside of your forearm, where there are no major blood vessels. Be bold! You may have to rush in while the knife arm is being pulled back to strike. This is very scary but you must do it with confidence and commitment, any half measures and you will get cut. You probably will get cut anyway, so try to ensure that it is nowhere vital.

The techniques for sticks and broken bottles, etc., are very similar to knife attacks. And with all the above, if you can conjure up an improvised weapon that will increase your chances.

DEFENCE AGAINST MULTIPLE ATTACKERS

The worst position for you is to be surrounded, so in this instance being in a corner is actually a good place to be. You must not let them take the initiative. This is where you really have to call on all your speed, aggression and surprise. If you get the opportunity, try to take out the leader or the toughest looking person first. That might give the rest of them pause. Manoeuvre yourself so that you are fighting one person at a time and the rest are getting in each other's way. This will work if they are not well organised or choreographed as in the next anecdote.

In my kung fu black belt training we had to fight multiple attackers and it was lots of fun. Surprisingly the hardest exercises we had were fighting just two lower belts who had been told to stand shoulder to shoulder, because as you tried to attack one, the other would attack you. The trick was to be as fast as possible and try to get them in line, so that you could deal with just one, kick them out of the way, and then

TOP TIP

In your training try as much as possible to replicate the kind of stress you would experience in a real situation, so do press-ups, sprinting, spinning round and round, and then get someone to attack you.

TOP TIP

You want to build up a conditioned response to an attack, and to do this you need to be under stress and then you MUST do all your punches, kicks, etc., with all your force – against pads of course.

start on the remaining fighter. There was always blood. We were very practised at pulling our punches normally but in that situation it is almost impossible and we used to damage the lower belts a bit. But then they were not as good at pulling punches, plus they would be a bit scared, so blood loss was usually about equal.

GRAPPLING

The philosopher's stone of self-defence is getting out of a police headlock and arm up the back combination. Several of us have come to the conclusion that until the philosopher's stone is found the best thing to do is to get out of the hold before it has been applied properly. There are lots of ways of getting out of all the other grabs, locks and holds, some of which use one or a combination of the following: punches, head butts, throws, joint manipulation, kicks and stamps.

DIY

Get along to self-defence classes; there are a few good ones about. Women particularly, seem to be well served with some excellent courses being run by committed feminist practitioners. When you have got an idea of what you are doing, why not get together as a group and go through some likely self-defence scenarios and work out your responses. Keep it as real as possible, short of hospitalising each other, so use rubber knives and lots of padding and really get stuck in. Enjoy.

FACT BOX

There have been many instances where very experienced black belt martial artists have been in street fights and done perfect punches to their attacker, but have pulled the punch because that is what they were used to doing in their training.

Survival Techniques

I'M A REVOLUTIONARY, GET ME OUT OF HERE

Survival is yet another of those words which have unfortunate connotations due largely to the, mainly American, right-wing sociopaths who seem to have made the term their own. I guess it is for this reason that the people who are genuine in their wish to live in closer harmony with nature and want to pass on their skills talk about Bushcraft and Woodlore. For us, though, survival is a more accurate term as we will be talking about living off the land for a relatively short space of time and, although perhaps not a matter of life and death, getting it right could mean the difference between freedom and incarceration.

We will only be using survival skills if things have gone wrong in a really dramatic way and we have to either take a very circuitous route to a RV or back to safety or we have to stay out of the way for a protracted period of time. If you have been training in a realistic fashion, then being alone in the wilderness should not be a great shock.

YOU CAN EAT THAT?

There is no point going in to great detail about survival techniques here as there are lots of available sources, some really good and some really bad ones. Most of the American Army Field Manuals are on the net including FM 21-76-1 which is the survival one. By far the most useful one I have ever read, and it is all about northern Europe, is called *Survival Advantage* by Andrew Lane. Ray Mears' books are great. *Food for Free* by Richard Mabey is justifiably a classic and there are lots of plant and edible fungi books about.

The purpose of this piece is to try to get you to remember everything you have learnt and put it into practice. The situation is bound to be a really stressful one, so a bit of state management is called for. You must initially seek to calm yourself and turn around the negative emotions you are bound to have. You can do this in seconds. Then you can start formulating your plans. Go through a tick list in your head. Do you have comms? Do you know exactly where you are and how to get to where you want to go? Do you have a compass and or map? Do you have a knife or any other equipment?

The first course of action should be to put as much distance between you and anyone looking for you as possible (even if this means initially heading away from where you want to go) – everything else is secondary. Escape and Evasion and Emergency Rendezvous are covered elsewhere.

Think about one of your members enrolling on a Bushcraft/Woodlore/Survival course. There are plenty about, look on the net and find a reputable sounding one near you.

PART FIVE

PARTY
GAMES

Part Five is about tactics, putting it all together: getting out there and using your skills of navigation to get you up close to the target, set up effective surveillance, complete the action and get back home at the end of it.

This will start to sound like a broken record but you have to practise, practise and then practise some more. When you are doing it for real you are going to be stressed and probably sleep-deprived, so try to duplicate that in your training. Go without sleep and maybe have one of your group attempt to sneak up on you, firing blank rounds, throwing fireworks, shooting at you with paint balls or BBs or popping flares to try and catch you out in the open.

Individual Camouflage and Concealment

"And what shall the poor girl wear, for all tomorrow's parties?" (Nico)

There are many topics covered in this book, the practice of which will make you feel ridiculous but none more so than the subject of Camouflage and Concealment (CC).

Putting on make-up, garnishing yourself with grasses and leaves, and crawling around the forest will, I'm sure, teach you a salutary lesson in humility.

Having said all that, it is vital that you pay attention to the detail of CC as it is that which, if you get it wrong, will give you away.

GOING GREY

They say that the art of camouflage (and it remains an art, no matter how much science they put into it) is 'not to be seen'. I say it is 'not to be noticed'. I think that the principles of CC can be extended to being the 'grey man' or 'grey woman' – being seen but not noticed.

Think about, for instance, the last time you were at the pub. If you were not too obliterated, think about the people in the pub. I bet you remember the ones you found attractive, obnoxious, menacing, loud, funny, mad, eccentric, strange-looking, disabled, very big or small, a different colour from the predominant one. Well forget about them now and try and describe the others – hard, huh? They are the grey men and women. When conducting recces, surveillance or actions, go grey. This is not as easy as it might at first appear, particularly if you are naturally flamboyant or extrovert. If you are tall, try to slouch a bit so that your height doesn't make you stand out. And it must be done right. Believe me, a charity shop, 1980s

> **The more he looked inside, the more Piglet wasn't there –**
> Winnie the Pooh

suit coupled with your bad hair cut and vegan friendly shoes will convince no one that you are a city gent.

Whoops, I feel an anecdote coming on. Although what I said above is true, sometimes a bit of arrogant self-confidence can overcome the limitations of your disguise.

Years ago I de-arrested a friend of mine on an action. She was being held by a cop and I walked over, held her by the arm and said, "I'll take her now" and off we went. My disguise was crap: white shirt, tie, Red Cross (I think) tunic which looked like a cop tunic apart from the buttons, black trousers and shoes. Oh! And my long hair tied back in a pony tail and tucked into my shirt. So how did I get away with it? I thought about that myself later and came to the conclusion that two factors were responsible. First, the white shirt, which made me a higher rank than the blue-shirted plod, and second, being on a high and knowing that I could do it. Dumb luck may have played a part but that cannot be relied on.

So, going back to the city gent example, if you can't pull that disguise off (and short of blowing a grand in Savile Row and visiting a good hair stylist, few of us can) then don't try. You will be more likely to pass as a janitor or tea lady.

You can sometimes get really good quality stuff from charity shops. Try the disguises out first in real situations and role play with each other.

Urban Camo

All the basics of CC are universal and apply to the urban environment as much as any other. They are:

- **Shape**: disguise yours;
- **Shadow**: try to keep in it;
- **Shine**: don't;
- **Silhouette**: don't make one by getting seen against a skyline (don't walk on ridges or rooftops, etc.);
- **Surface**: try to blend in with your surroundings;
- **Spacing**: if there are several of you keep spread out but not too regularly;
- **Movement**: move carefully – fast movement attracts attention.

You can add to these seven:

- **Noise**: make as little as possible; and
- **Smell**: no fags or Thermoses of curry.

There will be more on all this later.

FASHION FOR ACTION

Drab, dark colours are the obvious choice in an urban environment. Don't, in most circumstances, be tempted to wear military gear. Although military urban camo clothing has been developed to enable soldiers to blend into an urban environment, if you are seen wearing it you will really stand out, which rather defeats the object. Spend time observing what people actually wear in the target area (don't accept well known stereotypes) and dress in the prevailing fashion.

If, however, you are somewhere where you really must not be seen, then you will have to think about camming up. And, sorry, but although the Ninja look is really cool, plain black is not as effective as a camo pattern – you just look like the *shadow* of someone up to no good.

British camouflage is called Disruptive Pattern Material (DPM), which is a good name as the whole idea of CC is to break up your shape and disrupt the observer's perception of you and your equipment.

As we can't see colour at night (there will be more on this later in the Night Walking section), I think it is a moot point as to whether or not it makes much difference wearing a dedicated night time urban camouflage. So just use your normal DPM gear but make sure you buy fairly new genuine army surplus. The newer kit is Infra Red Reflective (IRR) (see Appendix ii), although it does wear out (and washing or even dry-cleaning combat jackets destroys their anti-infrared camouflage – so does starching, but I am sure this is an unnecessary warning). The clothing will help you defeat Infra Red (IR) detectors (more on this later).

DOES MY CROWBAR LOOK BIG IN THIS?

You will probably have to change into and out of or cover/uncover your camo gear quickly in an urban environment, so camo face paint is probably not an option. You will be wearing gloves anyway which will cover your hands and you could wear a balaclava, but that does give you the black blob, shadow of a head, ninja look again. I would recommend Spandoflage, which is probably best described as being a camo, close-knit, fishnet stocking. You can get it from army surplus outlets. Hats, scarves and glasses are also useful.

Rural Camouflage

Actions in rural areas give much more scope for effective CC and also, of course, for looking silly. Everyone should have a detailed understanding of recognition factors (what gets you noticed). The following factors are critical:

SKIN

Exposed skin reflects light and may draw attention. Even very dark skin, because of natural oils, will reflect light. CC paint sticks (available from surplus stores) cover these oils and help blend skin with the background. Don't use oils or insect repellent to soften the paint stick because it makes skin shiny and defeats the purpose. When you are putting on the cam cream it's a good idea to work in pairs and help each other – it's easy to leave gaps, such as behind ears, if you DIY. Here are some make-up tips to ensure you are the belle or beau of the action: paint high, shiny areas (forehead, cheekbones, nose, ears, and chin) with a dark colour. Paint low, shadow areas with a light colour. Paint exposed skin (back of neck, arms, and hands) with an irregular pattern. Day-old beard holds camouflage paint well. All puns resisted.

If Max Factor is not available use, in the jargon, field expedients such as burnt cork, bark, charcoal, lampblack, or mud. Mud contains bacteria, some of which is harmful and may cause disease or infection, so consider mud as a last resort. There is a dedicated product called 'Cam Off', or something like that, to remove the camo paint, but I'm sure that in the field Wet Wipes will do just as well, although they do smell a bit.

Remember hands.

CLOTHING

The DPM pattern on camo clothing often requires additional CC, especially when you are likely to be very close to the police/security. You can attach leaves, grass, small branches, or pieces of camo net to your clothing, and this will help distort your shape and blend with the natural background. As mentioned earlier camo clothing helps defeat visual and Near InfraRed (NIR) detection. Replace excessively faded and worn camo clothing because they lose their CC effectiveness as they wear. It is worth looking at publications such as Gun Mart, which often sells hunting camo, including ghillie suits at very good prices.

Carry elastic bands to attach foliage to yourself and your equipment.

MATERIALS

You should be using both natural and artificial materials for CC. Natural CC includes grass, bushes, trees and shadows. Artificial CC for people includes camo clothing, camouflage nets, camo skin paint, and natural materials. To be effective, artificial CC must blend with the natural background.

COLOUR

It is the contrast of skin, clothing, and equipment with the background which will get you seen. Your CC should blend with the surroundings or, at a minimum, you and your kit must not contrast with the background.

Study the nearby terrain and vegetation before applying CC to yourself or your equipment. During recces, analyse the terrain and then choose CC materials that best blend with the area. Change CC as required when moving from one area to another.

SHAPE

Use CC materials to break up your shape and stay in the shadows whenever possible, especially when moving, because shadows can hide you. When you have to get in close to the police/security, try to disguise or distort your body shape with artificial CC materials. Boots have a very distinctive shape and colour but are often overlooked – make sure you disguise them (see below).

MOVEMENT

Movement draws attention and can be detected by the naked eye, IR, and radar sensors. Minimise movement while in the open and remember that darkness doesn't stop you being seen by anyone equipped with modern sensors. When movement is necessary, slow, smooth movement attracts less attention than quick, irregular movement.

SHINE AND LIGHT

Shine can also attract attention. Pay particular attention to light reflecting from smooth or polished surfaces such as specks and watches (you can buy dedicated watch covers, make them yourself or just use gaffa tape or an elastic bandage – make the bandage dirty first or even dye it). Plastic map cases and clear plastic bags also reflect light. Red filters on flashlights, while designed to protect your night vision, are extremely sensitive to detection. Flashlights and lit cigarettes, bongs and pipes are equally observable. To reduce the chances of detection, replace red filters with blue-green filters (blue light is more difficult to see, but does not allow you to retain night vision) and practise strict light discipline. Use measures to prevent shine at night because moonlight and starlight can be reflected as easily as sunlight. Waterproof clothing, even the camo stuff, gets shiny when wet. You can get round this by wearing a waterproof under lightweight camo gear.

Winter Camouflage

PERSONAL CAMO
Personal winter camo is a fairly straightforward affair if you can get the German army over suit from an army surplus store. The suit is of a very lightweight nylon and is worn over your normal kit. The suit is reversible – completely white on one side for when there is total snow cover and white with pine needle type splodges on the other side for when the cover is only partial. With a white balaclava and gloves the effect is complete.

WINTER CONSIDERATIONS
There are a few considerations pertaining specifically to winter conditions, which are in addition to your normal safety and camouflage routine. Travel, by whatever means, is going to make lots of tracks. This can only really be avoided by travelling while it is snowing or when the wind is blowing snow around. These conditions will conceal your movement and cover your tracks.

Natural environmental and meteorological conditions during winter, particularly if travelling in mountainous terrain, could seriously damage your health. The extremely low temperatures, exacerbated by wind chill, can very quickly cause frostbite, hypothermia and death (see First Aid and Fitness sections). Avalanche and cornice collapse are also bound to ruin your day. It is vital that you know how to dress for the conditions and that you have winter experience gained in less stressful situations.

DISCIPLINE

Noise, movement, and light discipline contribute to your individual CC. Noise discipline muffles and eliminates sounds made by you and your equipment. Movement discipline minimises movement within and between positions and limits movement to routes that cannot be readily observed by others. Light discipline controls the use of lights at night. Avoid open fires, do not smoke in the open, and do not walk around with a lit flashlight.

THE BUDDY SYSTEM

"It's so much more friendly with two." (Winnie the Pooh)

Always use the buddy system of 'you check mine, I'll check yours', as mentioned above. It is useful when applying camo to make sure paint is applied completely (don't forget behind the ears); that extra camo materials are appropriate and in the right quantity; and that there are no reflective surfaces.

Finally, get your buddy to jump up and down to make sure they don't rattle. Water bottles should be completely full or completely empty so they don't make sloshing sounds as you move. Loose change is a no-no. If you are carrying coins for emergency phone calls, which is a good idea, tape them together or keep them in separate pockets.

Equipment Camouflage and Concealment

Camouflaging vehicles and equipment is covered in more detain in How They May Find Us. The vehicle question and many of the above considerations apply to camouflaging your equipment. Especially:

Shine and Light If you are trying to conceal a vehicle pay particular attention to light reflecting from smooth or polished surfaces such as windshields. Cover any shiny things you can or remove them from exposed areas.

Camouflage the shape of any other distinctive man-made objects. Tape all equipment that reflects light, such as mirrors and exposed metal objects. Tape your binocular lenses, allowing a slit opening for observation. Carry rubber bands for attaching natural camouflage to equipment. Carry extra pieces of camouflage netting to cover loose equipment. Camouflage any holes you dig when you set up an observation site. Holes should show no loose dirt. Cover plastic sandbags with soil or cloth. Run 'hard routine' (this is where you don't cook food and have light discipline: no fires, no cigarettes, no lights, and no illumination). One dead giveaway is:

Spoiled Camouflage Day-old leaves and branches wilt and discolour. Replace natural camouflage daily. Use a camouflaged poncho/basha as a cover to shade any light sources.

Night Work

BY THE LIGHT OF THE SILVERY MOON
Although this section is primarily about working at night, the information also applies to other times of limited visibility such as fog, rain and snow.

NIGHT VISION
Night vision works in a different way to day vision. At night, your eye uses spiral eye cells called rods. These cells can't differentiate colour, and are easily blinded when exposed to light. This creates a central blind spot, which causes larger objects to be missed, the more so as the viewing distance increases.

PROTECTING NIGHT VISION
Exposure to daylight directly affects night vision and repeated exposure to bright sunlight has an increasingly adverse effect on dark adaptation. Being out in intense sunlight for two to five hours causes a definite decrease in visual sensitivity which can persist for as long as five hours after exposure. So, although it is tempting to top up that tan and sunbathing can be very relaxing, try to wait until after the action. This effect can be intensified by reflective surfaces such as sand and snow. So, as with sunbathing, leave the day on the piste until after the action. Exposure to strong sunlight also means that the rate of dark adaptation and the degree of night vision capability will be decreased. Since these effects are cumulative and may persist for several days, sunglasses or goggles should be used in bright sunlight, particularly just before you expect to be involved in a night action/recce.

NIGHT VISION SCANNING
Dark adaptation or night vision is only the first step toward maximizing your ability to see at night. Night vision scanning enables you to overcome many of the physiological limitations of your eyes and reduce the visual illusions that so often confuse them. The technique involves scanning from right to left or from left to right using a slow, regular scanning movement. Although both day and night searches use scanning movements, at night you must avoid looking directly at a faintly visible object when trying to confirm its presence (see Bleach-Out Effect).

OFF-CENTRE VISION
Looking at an object using central vision during daylight is fine but this technique does not work at night. This is due to the night blind spot that is created when there are very low light levels. To compensate for this limitation, you should use off-

centre vision. This technique requires looking 10 degrees above, below, or to either side of an object rather than directly at it. This allows the peripheral vision to remain in contact with the object.

DARK ADAPTATION

Dark adaptation is the process by which the eyes increase their sensitivity to low levels of light and is what we call night vision. People adapt to the darkness to varying degrees and at varying rates. During the first 30 minutes in a dark environment, the eye sensitivity increases roughly 10,000 times, but not much further after that time.

Dark adaptation is affected by exposure to bright lights such as matches, flashlights, flares and vehicle headlights. Full recovery from this exposure may take up to 45 minutes.

Night vision goggles (NVGs) (see Appendix ii for more detail) impede dark adaptation. However, if your night vision has developed before donning the goggles, it will return about two minutes after removing them.

Colour perception decreases at night. Light and dark colours may be distinguished depending on the intensity of the reflected light.

Visual activity is also reduced. Since visual sharpness at night is one-seventh of what it is during the day, people can only see large, bulky objects.

BLEACH-OUT EFFECT

Even when you are using off-centre viewing the image of an object viewed for longer than two to three seconds tends to bleach out and become one solid tone. As a result, the object is no longer visible. To overcome this condition, you must be aware of this phenomenon and avoid looking at an object longer than two to three seconds. By shifting your eyes from one off-centre point to another, you can continue to pick up the object in your peripheral field of vision.

SHAPE OR SILHOUETTE

At night objects may have to be identified by their shape or silhouette. Try to get an idea of what the shapes of the structures common to the area of the action are like (this is another reason for conducting day-time recces before the night-time recce or action). For example, the silhouette of a building with a high roof and a steeple can be recognised as a church.

HOW TO SEE AT NIGHT WITHOUT NIGHT VISION GOGGLES (NVGs)

Try to learn what the restrictions on your night vision are and the cues for improving night vision (see above).

Always take the time to adapt to the dark, even if NVGs are going to be used. Don't wear a hood as it reduces both your field of view and your hearing. Using ordinary binoculars can radically improve your night vision. In moonlight, using your eyes alone you should be able to spot a person at 240 metres compared to 700 metres with binoculars. Scan continuously and avoid looking at an object directly. Don't use lights or illumination if it can be avoided. If it can't then remember that torches with red filters allow you to retain night vision. Try not to lose your night vision as it takes a long time to regain it; always close your eyes against lightning, flares, headlight, or other lights. If only one eye can be closed, that eye will maintain night vision because it occurs independently in each eye. Darkness affects visual acuity and distorts our vision: it modifies outlines, shapes, and colours so that shrubs look like people, fences can look like police or security patrols, and a village may look like a forest. Darkness also affects depth perception: height and distance are modified, dark objects appear farther away and light objects appear closer. Experience can increase your ability to perceive depth. On a clear night, you can recognise land relief up to 400 metres. At ranges less than 800 metres, people tend to underestimate range by as much as 25 percent. Haze, smoke, fog, overcast clouds and high humidity limit night observation.

There are lots of factors which hamper night vision, including fatigue. A tired set of eyes cannot see well and a tired observer is not mentally alert. For this reason you should rotate observation duty, with or without NVGs, every 30 minutes. Sleep is needed for night observation and you should try to get five hours per day minimum, six to eight hours per day is what you should be aiming for on long-term operations. Even 10 minutes of sleep can restore energy. Good physical fitness and stamina allows you to recover quicker. A lack of vitamin A, reduces night vision as does smoking because tobacco constricts blood vessels in the eye, reducing night vision by up to 20 percent. Booze as well is a no-no; drinking alcohol within 48 hours will slow your ability to acquire night vision. Alcohol impairs judgement, distance estimation, and coordination. Also if you are static it can lower your capacity to resist cold (see hypothermia in the First Aid section). Depression affects night vision and there are other medical problems which will mean that some people have less night vision capability than others. Presbyopia is the decrease in light transmission to the retina and is common in individuals over 40 years old. Night myopia affects nearsighted people and gives blurred vision at night. Astigmatism is an out-of-focus condition. An ordinary cold, and the narcotic medicine used to treat it, decreases night vision.

LIGHT SOURCES AND DISTANCES

This table shows the distances that light sources can be seen at night with the naked eye.

Sources	Distance
Vehicle headlights	4 to 8 kilometres
Bonfire	6 to 8 kilometres
Flashlight	Up to 2 kilometres
Lighted match	Up to 1.5 kilometres
Lighted cigarette	0.5 to 0.8 kilometres

For observation from the air, these distances can increase two to three times.

Night Walking

> "All truly great thoughts are conceived while walking." (Friedrich Nietzsche)

You will be approaching hides and surveillance sites at night so these are the techniques that you should get used to. You should train to move silently. Night movement requires the use of different muscles from day movement so you really must practice moving at night.

Before you do any serious night nav or movement you really need to have developed a high level of confidence and expertise. The only way to do this is to train hard. Areas such as the Brecon Beacons are an excellent proving ground for your talents (see Fitness section).

There is little point in getting into night nav until you have mastered day nav. As with all your training, night nav exercises should be progressive, leading up to multi-night long distance walks. You should do everything without resorting to your head torch. Start by using prominent features such as ridge lines (with, of course, the risk of walking off a cliff) and valleys, before moving on to more featureless terrain such as Dartmoor.

Bivi during the day, making sure that you cannot be seen. The training will also increase your general level of fitness, this is a must if you expect to outrun the cops or take part in extended actions or long surveillance.

Walking at night places more strain and exertion on the muscles of the thighs and buttocks as opposed to the calf muscles used for daylight travel. Night movement requires that these muscles become accustomed to taking short careful steps. The object is to make cross-terrain travel as natural as walking along a pavement.

Night walking proficiency is, like everything else, gained through practice. Here is a good way of walking at night. You begin by looking ahead, and then slowly lift your right foot about knee high. Balancing on your left foot, ease your right foot forward to feel for twigs, etc., with your toes pointed downward. Your foot should touch the ground about 6 inches in front of you then as the toes come to rest, feel for the ground with the outside of the toe of your boot. Then, settle your foot on the ground. As this step is taken, use your boot to feel for twigs and loose rocks.

 Confident of solid, quiet footing, slowly move your weight forward, hesitate, and then begin lifting your left foot. The process is repeated with the left foot. This method of balanced, smooth walking at night reduces the chances of tripping over roots and rocks and reduces noise. When you get used to moving at night, using the larger muscle groups of your legs you will be able to travel farther and with less fatigue.

How to walk silently at night

> "Always watch where you are going. Otherwise, you may step on a piece of the Forest that was left out by mistake." (Pooh's Little Instruction Book, Winnie the Pooh)

You should keep checking to make sure that you and your equipment are silent. Walk very slowly, trying to avoid all ground cover that makes noise. Use your equipment carefully to minimise noise and take plenty of rests. Rest between steps and tighten your socks and boots to make your feet more sensitive to objects on the ground. Use other sounds such as aircraft or vehicle noise to mask your movement. Muffle any coughs in the crook of your arm or use background noises to cover them, do the same when you need to clear your throat. Moving in the rain covers up a lot of the noise, the ground is soft, and it will be far more difficult for anyone to hear you. All scents are also washed away by the rain. The trade-off, however, is that your own ability to see, hear or smell is also gone.

A couple of things which will make you noisier are fatigue, as tired people are always noisy at night, and speed, because walking rapidly cannot be done silently unless you are on a clear, damp path. Even then, equipment noises usually increase.

One of the psychological problems associated with travelling at night is fear. Nyctophobia is an abnormal fear of night or darkness, but for many people apprehension rises significantly during darkness. The best way to overcome night time fear is just to spend more time out at night. Knowledge builds confidence. There are some very weird sounds in the great outdoors, but when you find out where they come from (the screeches of a barn owl; what appears to be the cries of someone being murdered but is in fact a fox, etc.) the fear goes. Unless, of course, you happen to be biviing on the Serengeti Plain, in which case it might be a blessing not to know what is making the noises.

> Don't underestimate the value of Doing Nothing, of just going along, listening to all the things you can't hear, and not bothering – Pooh's Little Instruction Book, Winnie the Pooh

ISN'T THIS ALL A BIT OVER THE TOP?

I don't think so. The reasons for such elaborate planning are that some of the targets we are interested in are out in the countryside. They are often well protected, have impressive security systems and operate, thanks to us, at a heightened level of paranoia. Because of the target's isolated position any observed incursions (your group on a recce/picnic) will ratchet up the paranoia level a couple of points. It will also, in the short term at least, mean that security will be tightened up and you may even be stopped and questioned. So, in the first instance, it is unlikely that you will be able to perform a detailed recce without these procedures, and if you do go ahead with an action, the chances of success and subsequent escape are lessened. A very high level of security cannot be maintained permanently, people are just not up to it, so if you do use these techniques you can catch them napping.

'The ghost walk' (see page 161)

Movement to Target Area

Joe Cabot: All right ramblers, let's get rambling! (*Reservoir Dogs*)

In this section it is assumed that you will need to approach your target across country. This may mean moving a couple of miles from where you have safely left your vehicle. In some cases, however, it may mean covering a much greater distance in order to be sure of avoiding detection. It may take more than one day to approach your objective, plus time for a thorough recce. With this in mind here are some techniques that will come in handy on a multi-day recce/action.

Before setting off you need to get your heads over a map and try to find concealed primary or alternate routes to the target.

> There is this to be said for walking: it's the one mode of human locomotion by which a man proceeds on his own two feet, upright, erect, as man should be, not squatting on his rear haunches like a frog –
> Edward Abbey

Spend as long as it takes on this. They should be selected based on detailed map and, if available, aerial photograph study; ground reconnaissance; and data on the target from other sources.

Obstacles such as rivers, thick forest, etc., should be looked at and plans for getting past, over or through them discussed. Treat populated areas as an obstacle because you will be moving tactically, in camouflage and would look highly suspicious if seen by members of the public.

SILHOUETTING

Make sure that your planned route is not along heavily populated routes or popular paths.

Try to make sure that you time getting into position for periods of reduced visibility and reduced alertness. The time is especially important during critical phases, e.g. when building hides, during surveillance, etc.

GPS

It is pros and cons time again. A GPS receiver can certainly be a very valuable tool. To start with you can use mapping software such as Anquet or Memory Map to plot your route on a computer. With some programmes you can even do a virtual, 3D walk through of your proposed route, giving you an idea of the terrain you are likely to encounter. You can mark waypoints, RVs and ERVs along the route and then download the whole thing into your GPS. Alternatively a group member could do a route recce during the day, keying in way points based on actual conditions on the ground. Equipment supplies, etc., could be cached along the way and their precise locations keyed into the unit. Alternate/escape routes could also be entered. Every one could carry a unit in case the group was split up or in case one or more of the units went down.

Now for the downside. GPS units are relatively expensive (although the price is coming down and even the cheapest unit will do everything you need). They are never a substitute for competent traditional navigation: batteries can fail (although if you don't have spares, well, don't get me started), you may not get reception in certain terrain (although this is much better now) and you might drop the unit over a cliff. But the number one negative is that if you are compromised and the unit is seized, you have effectively handed the cops your embarkation point, target, caches and most importantly the locations of RVs where the rest of the group might be. These issues have to be decided on a case by case basis.

Group members must know routes, RVs (and ERVs), time schedules and danger areas.

If you become aware of a police presence, you should try to move away undetected and maybe bin the action.

> "You can't stay in your corner of the forest, waiting for others to come to you; you have to go to them sometimes." (Winnie the Pooh)

Regardless of how you intend getting to the target area, the selection of the route is critical. Terrain, weather and man-made obstacles must all be considered when selecting the primary and alternate routes. The group can operate during reduced visibility by using night observation devices, if you can get them. Group members must maintain visual contact with each other; you can't afford to have anyone get lost. (The distance can expand and contract based on terrain and visibility.) This is a time when you should be really serious about maintaining noise and light discipline at all times. Each member should have their own area of responsibility. You should be moving along routes where you are shielded from observation. You should close up when you have to move through obstructions (darkness, smoke, heavy brush, narrow passes). If you have closed up to a single file, you should try to react in the same way as the member to your immediate front. You can open the formation up again when the obstructions to your movement and group communication lessen.

Movement Security

Everyone must be security conscious. You will have to maintain continuous all-round security as you need to be aware of all potential threats: a car coming along the road, torch lights, movement, voices, etc., in the distance, from any direction. When you are moving everyone will be responsible for an assigned security sector (left, right, front, behind). It is a good idea to make regular listening stops or when they are necessary. Keep checking that everyone's camouflage and that of the equipment is maintained at all times.

Packing

Follow the advice of the *Hitchhiker's Guide to the Galaxy* and always make sure you know where your towel (and everything else) is. The best way to ensure this, is to pack everything the same way every time. Make sure that the things you will be using first or needing most often are easy to get at and you've your compass, Maglight, etc., attached to you.

SUGGESTED GROUP KIT:

TOP ROW, LEFT TO RIGHT
1. Large Headtorch
2. Small Headtorch
3. GPS
4. Compass
5. Watch with wrist compass
6. Altimeter, barometer, compass
7. Altimeter, barometer, watch

BOTTOM ROW, LEFT TO RIGHT
8. Walkie-talkie in waterproof case
9. Penlight and case
10. Binoculars and case
11. Walkie-talkie in waterproof case
12. Walkie-talkie with press-to-talk kit

Arm-and-Hand Signals

GIVE US A WAVE

You will need to be able to communicate to each other silently and sometimes from a distance. The best way to do this is to use arm-and-hand signals. You can devise and adapt signals yourselves but I have illustrated a few useful ones to get you started.

Stop	Follow me	Close on me
Double (quickly)	Slow down	Lie down
Go back or turn around	Police/security seen	Looks good

Route Selection

Try to select a route that is easy to navigate, as night travel is strenuous and it is often done when people are tired, adding to the physical and psychological stress you are bound to be under anyway. Ease of navigation will contribute both to making sure you are going in the right direction and to keeping the group together. Have everyone following the route just in case you need to split up or if the main navigator gets geographically challenged. You will already have chosen the most likely covered routes to the target but, unless there are other reasons why you must move at a specific time, use a lunar calendar to determine the moon's direction, times and intensity. Then you can work out the most suitable time of the month and the best time of night to be moving. Remember that a full moon, while making it easier for you to navigate, will also make it easier for you to be seen. Similarly, bear in mind that thick cloud cover will obscure any moonlight; rain and wind will help you move unnoticed, dissuade security from being too vigilant on outside patrols, and in some instances will help cover your tracks (although it may also contribute to you leaving footprints). It is always a good idea to break up particularly long routes into legs and decide who will lead each leg. Determine distances, tick features, and catchment features. Don't depend solely on concealment, but a good covered route both conceals and protects. To stop silhouetting yourself, wherever possible select concave slopes to avoid horizons and don't use ridgelines. Always try to be aware of your background. Be conservative in selecting the length of the route – it will always take longer than you expect. Getting your group close to the target at night is slow and tedious, so don't overestimate the distance you are capable of travelling.

> "The atmospheric conditions have been very unfavourable lately," said Owl.
> "The what?"
> "It's been raining," explained Owl.
> "Yes," said Christopher Robin. "It has."
> "The flood level has reached an unprecedented height."
> "The who?"
> "There's a lot of water about," explained Owl.
> – Winnie the Pooh

RELOCATION, RELOCATION, RELOCATION

Recognisable terrain features such as hills, cliffs, rivers and ridges and man-made features such as towers, buildings, bridges and roads will all help your navigation.

A final ingredient is the reorientation plan; this is made considerably easier if you are using a GPS. Reorientation should be considered throughout the route (resections are discussed in the navigation chapter) and tickpoints, catchment features and handrails will all help with reorientation. Nevertheless, groups do get lost and this must be considered during the planning phase. You should have an idea of how to get back on track and complete the action. Think through 'getting lost' contingency plans during the reconnaissance and add extra legs if you think it necessary. By planning what to do if the group does get lost, the effects of actually getting lost are diminished.

Patience is the key to success. It will enable you to keep silent, move slowly and keep still for long periods. The human eye is very effective at detecting movement so try to move so slowly that an observer has difficulty seeing any movement. *Always assume you are being watched.*

Ministry of Silly Walks

Here are a few movement techniques. They look extremely silly but are very affective.

CRAWL

Stay as low as possible, wear gloves and kneepads if you need to (plumbers trousers are good as they come with removable knee protection), feel forward for any noisy obstructions or vegetation and try to make sure you are concealed from any potential observers.

DURING THE DAY USE:

Leopard Crawl

Keep flat to the ground, drag yourself forward with your arms and push yourself forward with your legs. This is a good method for crossing grass or very low cover.

Monkey Run

Crawl on your hands and knees behind low hedges.

AT NIGHT USE:

The Ghost Walk

Lift your legs high, sweeping them slowly outwards. Feel gently with your toes for a safe place to plant each foot, put your weight down gently; keep your knees bent. Use your left hand to feel the air in front of you from head height down to the ground checking for obstructions or alarms, etc. (see illustration, page 153).

The Cat Walk

Crawl on your hands and knees, search the ground ahead for twigs and move your knee to where your hand has searched.

Kitten Crawl

This is very quiet but it is also slow and very tiring. Lie on your front, search ahead for twigs, move them to one side. Lift your body on your forearms and toes, press forward and lower yourself to the ground.

OTHER THINGS TO CONSIDER

Lose your shape

Avoid skylines

Use cover

Use local vegetation

Roll away from a ridge or skyline to avoid being silhouetted.

ABOUT FLARES (NOT THE SCARY BELL BOTTOMS)
Freeze if you have time after hearing the 'pop' of an illumination flare, back up one step and quickly lay down. Close your eyes to retain night vision. Close just one eye if you need to be able to see.

You should get used to tuning into all your senses, particularly at night. Similarly you need to protect yourself from being detected in the same way.

Hearing

Your hearing becomes more acute at night. There are probably several factors that contribute to this: increased concentration, the fact that sound travels farther in colder, more moist air and the absence of background noise. Practice and training help overcome your fear of what you hear at night (despite noises to the contrary, there are no tigers prowling the Cotswolds). Training enables you to discriminate between multiple sounds, faint sounds, and sound source directions. The table below shows the distances that sounds can be heard at night.

Sources	Distances
Motor Vehicle movement	
On a dirt road	Up to 500 metres
On a main road	Up to 1kilometres
Movement on foot	
On a dirt road	Up to 300 metres
On a main road	Up to 600 metres
Metal on metal	Up to 300 metres
Conversation of a few people	Up to 300 metres
Steps of a single person	Up to 40 metres
Axe blow and sound of a saw	Up to 500 metres
Blows of shovels and pickaxes	Up to 1,000 metres
Screams	Up to 1,500 metres
Oars on water	Up to 2,000 metres

HOW TO LISTEN AT NIGHT

Stand still, be silent, cup both of your hands around the back of your ears. Face in the direction of any sounds and scan your head from left to right. Close your eyes to better focus your senses on the sounds. Don't wear a hood, as it reduces your hearing ability. Don't cover your ears with a woolly hat (it's cute and your aunt spent an awfully long time knitting it, but just don't, okay). Learn the normal background sounds. Note the absence of crickets and birds. Listen for man-made sounds, especially metal on metal, which are really distinctive in the field.

HOW TO AVOID BEING HEARD

Silence yourself and your equipment. Pack all your kit in a functional manner so that you know where everything is and can noiselessly retrieve it at night. Avoid wearing noisy waterproofs (a good way to deaden the noise, cover the shine of a wet waterproof and cover the

TOP TIP

Open your mouth. You might start to drool, but it will cut out the sounds of your pulse and your breathing – try it.

colour of a bright waterproof is simply to wear a thin camo jacket over the top). Vegetation catching on the waterproof makes noise. Turn off all watch alarms and mobile phones. Run radios in squelched mode and minimise their use. Click handset send button twice for 'yes' and once for 'no.' Velcro is wonderful in so many ways but it is noisy. If you have Velcro on clothing or equipment consider covering it. Do the jumping up and down test – it will keep you warm and you will hear if you have any jingly things about your person.

Smell

A ROSE BY ANY OTHER NAME...

Smell is your most underused sense; in fact only about two percent of its potential is used. As I'm sure you will have noticed, different diets produce different characteristic human odours. People who eat a meat diet have a different body odour than people who eat a vegetarian/vegan diet. Did you know that your diet can even be detected in a sample of your hair? Once you are accustomed to a characteristic odour, that smell is easy to detect and differentiate at night.

Practice will improve your skill and confidence. Your capability to pick up a scent at night can be improved by facing into the wind at a 45-degree angle. You should relax, breathe normally, take sharp sniffs, think about specific odours, and concentrate.

Diesel fuel can be sensed up to 500 metres away and cigarette smoke up to 150 metres. Smoky fires (usually the result of burning wet or green wood) can be detected farther still. Fish, garlic and other foods being cooked can be smelled several hundred metres away.

LEARN TO SMELL

Stop. Close your eyes to focus your senses on smell. Lift your nose and smell in all directions. Teach yourself the smells of the environment. Smell sap from recently cut tree branches. Smell soil from newly turned earth. Avoid smoking cigarettes and second-hand smoke – it interferes with your ability to smell. Don't ruin your sense of smell prior to an action. You will have noticed, from miles away, the pong of aftershave and cheap scent of people going out on the raz on a Friday night. So, even if you think your particular fragrance is rather more subtle than the bargain box at Boots, bin the scented soap, after-shave, and newly laundered clothes – it's as powerful as Old Spice on the hill. The same goes for soap, shaving cream, toothpaste and insect repellent.

Avoid being Smelled

While moving to the target, particularly if it takes many hours or even days, we are going to need to pee and poo and we do not want the smell to alert the cops to our presence. So, get the embarrassed sniggers out of the way, pull out your copy of *How To Shit In The Woods*, this is how to do it:

PEEING

Try to find some loose earth and dig a hole with your heel, piss into the hole and cover it with earth. Avoid the Indian before an action as spicy foods give a distinctive odour to urine. Kneel to pee, it shortens the distance to the ground thus minimising noise. Aim at a leaf or bush to make less sound. Vegetation absorbs urine and minimises smell. Loose earth and vegetation absorb noise. Urine stains on rocks are visible and smell when warmed by the sun. Don't use toilet paper, of course, both sexes will just have to give a good shake to get rid of the drops.

POOING

Entrenching Tool for Digging Holes

As above select a low site with good earth and good ground cover. Take care with site selection as wind blowing across poo holes on high ground can carry the smell far downwind. Use low ground and shit more than 50 metres from running water. Dysentery can result from unwashed hands and utensils – not much fun if you are in a hide. Put toilet paper, if you must use it, in your pocket to stop it blowing away, keep your equipment at arm's length and dig your hole. Straddle the hole and squat with your trousers and pants pulled forward (this is vital if you don't want to fill your pants – watch out for your trouser bottoms as well). After you have wiped, put the used tissue paper in the hole. Be careful not to let your toilet paper blow away – toss some soil on each piece of paper as you place it in

the hole. Fill in the hole with earth and replace any ground cover to camouflage it. Wash your hands or use a wet wipe. Minimise the smell by burying all excrement immediately. You can use an anti-diarrhoeal like Immodium to avoid having to crap in the short term. Army rations are also known to make you constipated. This is not recommended by doctors, but can be used on certain actions of fairly short duration. Carrying excrement in plastic bags out of the area of operations (this is mainly for when you are involved in surveillance and you have to spend a lot of time in a hide) is a good idea. Certain actions may require this to avoid evidence of activity.

GREEN BOX

If the tactical system allows, always be aware of the environmental effect of shitting. Dig your hole 50 metres away from water courses (for peeing, 20 metres away), make the hole six inches deep and use natural materials (moss, leaves) rather than toilet paper. If you do use paper, burn it or carry it away with you.

Toilet Paper
There is no real reason to use paper. Just apply a liberal amount of Vaseline to your bum hole before you go and your jacksy will remain clean as a whistle. If you insist on using it, be economical and only use three sheets of paper – one up, one down, one shine.

Poo Bagging
There are several ways of doing this, but one of the most economical is to crap onto a piece of clingfilm, wrap the jobbie up and double bag it to keep it airtight. It is, of course, a good idea to practise this before you need to do it for real. You may need the help of a friend – it is a good way to find out who they are.

WASHING
Dig a small hole with the heel of your boot. Wash, and brush teeth so that all the water drains into this hole. When you have finished cover the hole with earth and replace the ground cover to camouflage it. When you are going to stay in one place for a while, a single wash area should to be set up to minimise smell.

COOKING AND EATING

Some Considerations
Warm food certainly smells more than cold food, so only cook when absolutely necessary. Jetboil stoves (see the pictures on the next page) are the business for

boiling water – the flame is hardly visible, they are super fast and don't make too much noise. Tabasco sauce smells (sad but true).

Unless you are in a survival situation, you should not light fires. Not only do they smell but they also produce smoke. If you have to light a fire don't use green wood or leaves and build them in holes. Don't cook at all (hard routine) when you are in close proximity to your target.

"And we must all bring Provisions."
"Bring what?"
"Things to eat."
"Oh!" said Pooh happily. "I thought you said Provisions. I'll go and tell them."
And he stumped off. (*Winnie the Pooh*)

Sleep

TO SLEEP, PERCHANCE TO DREAM

As has been noted sleep is vital, so always try to find a good place to kip. Step the ground to find roots or rocks, roll your kip mat out and lie on it to test the ground, roll your sleeping bag out then repack your rucksack. If I am using a bivi bag, I always have my sleeping bag already inside it. It's less faff, and if it is raining, it will protect the sleeping bag. If you are using a bivi bag, it is vital that you make sure that you remove any brambles or anything sharp from the ground before you put it down. You will be getting into your sleeping bag with dirty clothes and boots. So to prolong the life of your bag and prevent you having to wash it so often, it is worthwhile having a sleeping bag liner. You can get Pertex or silk ones that weigh virtually nothing and dry really quickly. Fleece liners are also available which effectively add an extra season's warmth to your bag.

When you choose a sleeping bag(s) for a particular action you have to make several choices. Sleeping bags are basically either down or synthetic.

Down is, weight for weight, very much warmer than synthetic and packs down much smaller, but it is more expensive. Generally the more you pay, the better quality down you get. The big disadvantage of down though is that when wet it loses most of its thermal properties and becomes a heavy soggy mess which takes an age to dry out. So only use down in dry climates, when sleeping in a tent or if you are feeling lucky. I wouldn't even use them in a bivi bag in case of leaks.

Synthetic bags have improved massively in the last few years and they are getting closer to the performance of down. One of the big developments came because the US military demanded a superior bag and Primaloft was developed. Now many other manufacturers have started to produce their own excellent products.

When you select a bag you should know if you are a warm or a cold sleeper, and in what conditions you are going to use the bag. Unless you are planning on scaling an 8,000 metre peak, you are not going to need an extreme bag. I have used one season, i.e. summer, bags for sleeping in snow holes in Scotland – and remember you can wear all your warm clothes. You should never need more than a good three season bag in the UK. The ideal would probably be to have a one season bag and a three-season bag and, if you are a cold sleeper or are going to be somewhere really cold, you can combine the two. You should choose your bag in a tactical colour or make sure it is always covered by your bivi bag.

You may have to bug out with very little notice so keep all your gear at arm's length, packed and ready. Use your jacket as a pillow. If there is a really good chance you will have to leave in a hurry, then keep your boots on. Otherwise take them off and put loose items from your trouser pockets in them. Cover your boots up to keep beasties out. Loosen your trousers and socks. All you snorers should sleep on your stomachs – nothing to do with security, it just sounds awful. Always know where your gear is and how to retrieve it silently in the dark. Take only the equipment you need. Don't spread your equipment around, you're not at home now. You should be able to grab your gear with two hands and move out.

For one-night actions you can afford to rough it, to save weight and fuss, but for anything longer, it is worth carrying a kip mat for effective sleep. For training I use a ¾ length Thermarest, which is an inflatable mat, but for actions you don't want anything that can get punctured. You should use a closed cell foam mat. All you need is a ¾ length to protect your torso from the cold ground; you can place your rucksack under your legs to protect them. Cut your mat down to size and taper it down from your shoulders. I always find lots to do with the cut off sections. But that's me, give me some closed cell foam, an inexhaustible supply of gaffer tape and I'm a happy man.

Military style rucksack from
Karrimor and Berghaus

Bivi bags under basha

All this kit should be attached to your jacket

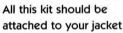

Binoculars

Compass

Torch and multi-tool

Camera in solid waterproof case

How to Build a Poncho/Basha Hooch

A basha (an army surplus issue basha costs about £35) is a camo tarp which has grommets or webbing loops around its edges and in the centre, and is easy to use for making a shelter. It is an incredibly versatile bit of kit and you can configure it

in lots of different ways so that it could look like a ridge tent, a tepee or a lean-to. The design will vary depending on what you are attaching it to: trees, fences, walls, etc. Obviously the closer you build it to the ground the less chance of detection there is. I have found that a combination of varying lengths of bungees with hooks and twizzle pegs (all green, of course) works best. If you are using a camo poncho, tie off the neck of the poncho with its drawstrings (to stop rain getting in), then tie

each line to separate trees or other vegetation, creating a lean-to shelter facing into the wind. Always carry a couple of spare bungee cords. Avoid drainage areas if rain is expected.

HOW TO AVOID SLEEPING WHILE STANDING WATCH AT NIGHT (STAG)
Stand or walk to stop yourself dozing and drink coffee/Red Bull or take caffeine pills. It is vital that you stay awake. If the tactical situation prevents you standing, then kneel, don't sit. That way if you do go to sleep, you will fall and wake up. Make sure you know the sleeping position of your relief. If you need to check map, notes or equipment, spread your poncho/basha on the ground and crawl under it making sure that the edges remain flush to the deck. Always use a red-lens flashlight to protect your night vision. You can get more than one head under the poncho/basha if you need to have a meeting. Someone should watch outside to make sure that no light escapes. Don't allow yourself to be over-confident, as there is no safe technique for fires, cigarettes or flashlights. Only use this trick for flashlight checks of maps or equipment, and only when you really need to, as unpacking, spreading out, using, and repacking a poncho/basha creates plenty of unwanted noise. And don't try to use it to cover up fires. D'uh!

FATIGUE
Fatigue is the result of too much work with too little sleep and it has a negative impact on a group's capability in a high stress situation. You can avoid fatigue to a great extent if you can develop an effective work-rest schedule that ensures recovery time so that the group's effectiveness is maintained. The following are some techniques to minimise fatigue. A four-hour-on, four-hour-off stag works well in most situations, but if the weather is bad try two hours on and four hours off. Other stag schedules may work as well and none suit everyone, but a specific schedule might work best for most of the people in a certain group. Try various methods to find which one works best. Be sure people sleep or rest during part of each off-shift period. Make sure that everyone has been trained in all the different tasks so that they can rotate through various duties to reduce errors. You should have two people for each job requiring decision making. Order of priority of sleep should be decided in terms of seriousness of errors, complexity of tasks, and tedium of duties. Some people are more efficient early in their awake cycle; others later on. Try to capitalise on the decision makers' best times for their critical task (this should be planned).

Night Time Signals

I HEARD IT THROUGH THE GRAPEVINE
The arm-and-hand signals we looked at earlier work fine during the day but may not be visible during darkness. At night you can use signals to pass information, identify locations or initiate activity.

The key to tactical communications is simplicity, understanding, and practice, so signals should be as simple as possible to avoid confusion. Understand and, guess what, practise each basic signal and its alternate (if necessary).

SEE ME, HEAR ME, TOUCH ME...
The most common signals relate to the senses: hearing, feeling and seeing. Audio signals include radio, telephones, messengers, and grating or clicking objects together. Messengers should carry written messages (rather than using the Chinese whispers technique where 'the police are behind the wall on the right' becomes 'two portions of chips and a warm rabbit') to avoid confusion and misinterpretation. When this is not possible, ensure the messenger understands the message by having them repeat it word for word.

HOW TO DO ORAL
Oral communication at night should be whispered. To do this, take a normal breath, exhale half of it, and then whisper into the other person's ear using the remainder of the breath.

When using the radio and phone at night, operators should take precautions, lowering the volume as low as practical, using headphones or earphones to reduce unnecessary noise and using signals (such as breaking squelch a specified number of times, e.g. once for no, twice for yes). Remember that noise travels farther at night than during the day.

VISUAL SIGNALS
There are visual alternatives to audio signals that you can use, but they are only useful if they are noticed and recognised.

Some passive signals are things like sticks indicating direction, paint, tape, rock formations, markings on the ground and powder. Active signals include flares, flashlights, chemical lights (glow sticks), infrared strobe lights, normal strobe lights, burning fuel (saturated sand in a can), luminous tape or a compass dial.

You can use these signals to identify a critical path junction, mark a rendezvous point, mark caches, or report that a danger area is clear. White powder can be used to indicate direction at a confusing path intersection. A flashlight with a blue filter (with an X cut out of the filter) can signal all clear to a group crossing a danger area. The possibilities are endless, but, ensure that each signal used is understood by each person in the group. Remember, if you can follow signals, so can others.

LET'S PLAY FOOTSIE

The last type of signal is the sense of touch. You may use wire, string, or rope to communicate without fear of disclosing your position. The wire is usually loosely tied to your arm or leg. This may be a useful technique to use in the hide or surveillance positions. It will not be possible to develop a complex language or even a simple one that you can use in every situation (tug the string 146 times for 'I've got to take a leak'? I don't think so). You need to be using pre-arranged signals for the vital things you are likely to need to communicate on that particular action. The information is relayed from one person to another so, regardless of the type of signal used, it must be simple, easy to understand, and practised.

Reconnaissance

OF HIDE AND SURVEILLANCE SITES

"Sometimes, if you stand on the bottom rail of a bridge and lean over to watch the river slipping slowly away beneath you, you will suddenly know everything there is to be known." (Pooh's Little Instruction Book – Winnie the Pooh)

Surveillance on a target is a vital part of planning an action and it must be done with care. Before you get into the elaborate preparations detailed below, see if it would be possible to use a remote camera. If not, the first thing to get right is the site of your surveillance and hide positions. The tentative hide site, surveillance site(s) and routes to them you will have selected during the planning phase from maps and aerial photographs. It is vital that you do a daytime recce of the site to make sure it is suitable and, if possible, that the target can be observed from the site at ground level. The recce should be made during a period of limited visibility, for instance when it is raining. The people who have done the recce should brief the remainder of the group on the site and together you should make an occupation plan.

SITE SELECTION
When you are considering a site, look at the following aspects: Does the position have a good line of sight to the target? Does it have adequate overhead concealment and cover? Is it away from roads, paths, railway tracks and major waterways? Can you set up good primary and alternate exits for if you need to leave in a hurry? Can you make a concealed, serviceable entrance where people and kit can get in without being seen? Will it be possible to get into and out of the hide site without making much noise? Is it near man-made objects? Is it downwind of inhabited areas? Can it be sited so that it is not dominated by high ground, but takes advantage of the high ground? Can you place the target under continuous and effective observation with the range of surveillance devices you have? Will the surveillance site have to move if weather and light conditions change? Does the area provide concealment and entrance and exit routes? Are there dominant or unusual terrain features nearby? Is the area wet, is there adequate drainage, or is the

area prone to flooding? Are there other natural lines of movement nearby (gullies, any terrain easy for walkers)? Could the group be easily trapped in the site? Are there any obstacles to prevent vehicle movement nearby (roadside ditch, fence, wall, stream, river)? Are there any suitable communication sites nearby? Is the site in the normal line of vision of the target or local people? Is there a source of water in the area?

DECISION TIME
It is only when you have answered the above questions that you can make an informed decision about the viability or otherwise of a particular site. It is highly unlikely that you will ever have the perfect site and you are going to have to place several factors in the balance. Ultimately there are just two major considerations. First, will surveillance from this site provide you with all the information that you need for planning the action, e.g. movements, security levels, etc? Secondly, is there a very good chance that you will be able to pull off the level of surveillance you need without being spotted yourself? If you are happy with the answers you can go ahead with the next stage – construction and occupation.

Hide and Surveillance Sites

CONSTRUCTION AND OCCUPATION

Types of Hide and Surveillance Sites

There are obviously lots of possible designs for the hide and surveillance sites, many of which will be dictated by the terrain but there are two main categories of site that you are likely to use. They are the surface site and the hasty sub-surface site. Always watch and listen before starting any construction work on the site(s).

The hide and surveillance positions can be in the same location. The difference is that the hide site provides a base from which to stage communications (either a remote communication site – you might have to do this to get a mobile signal – or directly from the hide site). It reduces the number of people at the surveillance site and, as it will be out of the line of sight to the target, it will reduce the chance of being spotted. The hide site will be the group's base and members of the group can be rotated to and from the surveillance site. The surveillance site is where selected group members observe or survey the target. Communication between the two sites should be by radio or messenger. If the surveillance is going to be for a relatively short period or if the area is just too sensitive to have people moving around, you will just have to dispense with the hide site.

Surface Site

Hasty surface sites are used when the group plans to be in occupation for a short period (generally less than six hours) and the group should make the best possible use of natural cover and concealment. Use man-made camouflage materials as required to improve concealment. Keep movement to a minimum. Generally, two or three members are positioned forward to observe the target area and record information. The hasty hide site is positioned far enough to the rear so it is out of the direct line of observation. The distance will normally depend on terrain and vegetation, but it must be far enough away from the surveillance group so that, if one of the two elements is discovered by police/security, the other element has enough stand-off (distance) to prevent them from being discovered too. The group members in the hasty hide site will be in charge of maintaining security for the rear and sides. Communication is normally conducted after the group moves away from the area.

The advantages of a surface site are that it is easy to construct, requires a minimal amount of materials, can be done quickly and quietly, no large amounts of soil need to be relocated and the surveillance group can escape quickly (but there is a risk of compromise by dogs and walkers).

For construction you can use waterproof ponchos or bashas, camouflage net (which prevents reflection from the poncho/basha and aids in camouflage), para cord or bungee cord, chicken wire, burlap or canvas cloth. A folding saw is very useful for cutting small branches. The precise construction details will depend on the terrain, the likelihood of getting sussed, whether you need 360 degree observation and many other factors. But the basic considerations are: is there much vegetation about, bushes, etc? If so the site can be above ground and you can use the natural vegetation combined with your bashas, etc., to blend into the landscape. If there is no vegetation then you will have to dig a shallow scrape to lie in and cover it with a basha, camo net, etc.

You should avoid cutting any fresh vegetation for camouflage as it shows up. Remember to keep all your equipment packed when not in use just in case you have to do a runner. Security must be maintained 24 hours a day. You will have to strike a balance between the effectiveness of the surveillance (with three group members, you can stay longer and one group member can rest) and the likelihood of the site's discovery (with three people, the site is larger and harder to conceal.) The best time to switch surveillance groups is just after dark and just before daylight.

In some situations, surveillance of the target may only be done during limited visibility and the group must stay in the hide site during the day. The surveillance site must have all-round coverage, with nets or natural camouflage so it cannot be seen from any angle including overhead. The distance between the hide site, the surveillance site and the communication site (if used) depends on various factors, terrain being the main one. The group should change directions when moving from the hide site to the surveillance site, when possible (dog leg, fish hook, or indirect route). The group should not wear gillie suits (this is camouflaged clothing covered with strips of Hessian to further break up your shape during movement). Pieces of the suit will rip off in vegetation and leave a path. If you use them, put the suits on just before occupying the surveillance site.

Hasty Sub-surface Site
A hasty sub-surface site is constructed when the surveillance is going to take a long time, e.g. where you need to watch the comings and goings at a target on every day of the week. A complete sub-surface site would be a very unlikely option. The hasty site is especially useful when there is little natural cover and concealment. The site is planned so that it could be improved to a full sub-surface site as time and the situation allows, although this is very unlikely to be necessary. This type of site has a lower profile than the surface surveillance site and excellent camouflage,

but it does have downsides. For instance, it involves digging with only entrenching tools, the soil must be concealed, it requires more time to construct and there will be some level of construction noise. And one of the biggest downsides is the problem of getting all the kit to the site.

You can use poncho/bashas or other waterproofing; small camouflage net to assist in camouflage; entrenching tool (this is a folding shovel); para cord or bungee cord; chicken wire (optional); burlap or canvas (optional); sandbags; PVC pipe with connectors; fibreglass rod; aluminium conduit; plywood (get down to B&Q).

Hi Ho, Hi Ho
While building the observation position, try and camouflage it as you go and carefully dispose of earth spoil. Carefully cut and then roll back turf before you start digging. Remember that too much camo material applied to a position can actually have a reverse effect and disclose the position. Collect all the vegetation you are going to use for camouflaging the site from around quite a wide area to avoid drawing attention to the position by the stripped area around it.

To avoid disclosing your position, never leave shiny or light-coloured objects exposed – that includes removing your shirts to get a tan on your pasty white bodies. Don't use fires, leave tracks or other signs of movement. Don't look up and wave when aircraft fly overhead. (One of the most obvious features on aerial photographs is the upturned faces of people.) When the camouflage is complete, inspect the position from police/security's viewpoint. Check CC periodically to see that it stays natural-looking and conceals the position. When camo materials become ineffective, change or improve them.

Avoid Being Seen
As before, camouflage the shape of distinctive man-made objects and tape all equipment that reflects light. Camouflage any holes you dig when you set up an observation site and make sure that no loose dirt from the holes can be seen. If you are using plastic sandbags cover them with soil or cloth. Run 'hard routine'. (This is where you don't cook food and have light discipline: no fires, no cigarettes, no lights, and no illumination.) One dead giveaway is spoiled camouflage. Day-old leaves and branches wilt and discolour, so replace natural camouflage daily.

Actions In The Hide Site
It is important that the group is really switched on; you must maintain security at all times. It is a good idea to sit either back-to-back or feet-to-feet, using all-round security. You should always wait about 15 minutes before moving or unpacking equipment, using this time to listen and tune into the environment. Don't lean

against small trees or vegetation as these inadvertent Laurel and Hardy moments may have serious consequences. Have your kit with you at all times in case you need to bug out in a hurry. Camouflage all around the position. The best time to rotate shifts is at dusk and dawn and you should then try and rest during the day.

> "It is more fun to talk with someone who doesn't use long, difficult words but rather short, easy words like 'What about lunch?'" (Pooh's Little Instruction Book – Winnie the Pooh)

Priority of Work

Work priorities may vary, with the exception of security, which is always a priority. The group should already have formed security, alert, evacuation and rendezvous plans. The group should conduct stand-to (stand-to is when every one is in a high state of awareness and takes place at times of greatest threat), starting before first light and continue it until after full light. And then another stand-to, starting before dark and continuing until after dark. Try to vary the exact starting times to keep from setting a pattern. It may be a good idea to select and recce alternate hide and surveillance sites – just in case. Make sure that your equipment, radios and camouflage are all in good order.

FEATHER DUSTER TIME

Before leaving the hide and surveillance locations, you must make sure that the sites and routes have been sterilised. Carry out all the stuff you brought in, including waste and rubbish, rather than burying it if possible. Animals will almost certainly find your trash and dig it up. If rubbish has to be buried it should be 18 to 24 inches deep in sealed containers (the BDH bottles used for canoeing are good for this). Alternatively cover the scent by using lime. Sterilise the sites using displaced earth and use the site to bury any material which contrasts with the surrounding area. Camouflage the whole area by blending the site with its surroundings. As you withdraw from the site, ensure that your routes are camouflaged to prevent detection (brushing branches over the route, scattering leaves etc).

THE ARTS OF SUFFERING AND BOREDOM

> "Rivers know this: there is no hurry. We shall get there some day."
> (Winnie the Pooh)

Surveillance is uncomfortable. You are likely to be cramped, cold and wet for lengthy periods of time and, if you are doing a solitary surveillance, you will be lonely as well. Even if your mates are with you, you won't be able to talk to them properly so expect a rough time of it. The main way to go about doing surveillance as a group is from a hide or surveillance site. Sometimes the terrain, action and location of the site may dictate that you establish a separate surveillance site to effectively observe the area. This means splitting the group, exposing yourself to a greater chance of being spotted and using extra equipment, but it may be the price you have to pay to make sure you get all the surveillance data you need.

Be tight with keeping up noise, light, litter and odour discipline at all times. The group must keep movement (day and night) to an absolute minimum and talk only in whispers. You should normally communicate using your arm-and-hand signals. However, if this is impractical because of, for instance, distance and vegetation, use a messenger or the radios. You should have a minimum of two people (I will discuss single person surveillance later) to conduct effective surveillance. One observes while the other records the information in the surveillance log. (Don't let this fall into the hands of the police. D'uh!) Because observer efficiency decreases rapidly after half an hour, the observer and the recorder should switch duties about every 30 minutes. If you are using night vision devices, the observer's initial period of viewing should be 10 minutes followed by a 15-minute rest period. After several periods of viewing, the period can be extended to 15 and then to 20 minutes. Those in the hide site should be rotated every 24 hours. During periods of limited visibility, when it might be difficult to see what is going on with the target, two to three (normally three) members may be required to set up a new surveillance site. This new site should be nearer the target area so that information may be collected through close-in observation and sound detection. The remainder of the group should stay in the hide site. You will have sussed out this possible extra surveillance site and the route to and from it during your recce, in daylight. Members need to go in and out of the surveillance site during limited visibility. One member observes, one records, and one maintains security to the rear and flanks (sides). Only passive night vision devices (see Appendix ii) should be used, to help prevent detection.

Single Person Surveillance

This is real DIY and has its own pros and cons. On the plus side you only have to worry about yourself; there is no one else around to make a noise; the site is going to be much smaller and therefore harder to detect; there will have been less movement and disturbance getting there and it is easier to be flexible as to site setting, etc. On the negative side there is no one to look to for support; you can't get someone else to check your concealment and continuous surveillance cannot be carried out, so it is only suitable for surveillance of a few hours or when you only need to keep a lookout at certain times of the day (which means that you can get some kip at other times).

BACK TO THE TREES

The possibilities for concealment really open up if there is only one person who has to be hidden. Here are a few suggestions for a one person observation post (OP). What better surveillance site could there be than up a tree? You would have a bird's eye view – no need to worry about high fences blocking your line of sight. You would be unlikely to be detected by a casual passer-by as people rarely look more than a couple of feet above their own eye level. Dogs would not piss on you or dig you out.

The Perfect Tree

There are numerous considerations when looking for the perfect tree. The only type of trees that would be suitable are deciduous – you would slide out of a conifer, always assuming you could get through the dense foliage in the first place. But of course this type of leaf shedding tree would be useless in winter. The tree must have enough foliage to conceal you, but afford you an unhindered view of the target. You will probably need a certain amount of extra equipment to climb the tree (see section on Tree Stirruping and Prussiking) and to secure yourself in it. It is likely to be pretty uncomfortable and if you are sussed you can't just run away. It goes without saying that, apart from a daytime walk past to select the tree, you will be doing all the work at night.

The Perfect Bush

How about the perfect bush? There is probably no such thing, as the two most likely bushes you are going to find yourself in are either gorse or bramble, so it is going to be a prickly experience. But if trees, for whatever reason, are not an option look for a nice, bushy bush. It will probably take some time to decide if you have a good one. Have a casual walk past in daylight to see if there is a thick bush with at least a possible line of sight to the target. With gorse or bramble you are almost certainly going to need to 'improve' the bush, this will involve the use of secateurs and possibly a folding saw.

HOW TO SET UP A ONE PERSON OBSERVATION POST

First stash all the kit you will not be using to construct the hide, away from the site. Cut into the bush so as to give just enough space for you and your kit. Don't forget that if it is a multi-day surveillance you will need enough room to have a poo (unless you have been popping Immodium). Peeing, for men at least, can be done into a bottle while lying down. Wear gardening gloves to prevent your hands getting trashed. Make sure that there is an uninterrupted line of sight for your camera (you will want a small tripod – remember that digital cameras don't have shutters, so are silent) or binoculars to the target (it is hard to be sure at night). Check to see if you are able to get phone or radio contact from the site. Unless the bush is incredibly dense, you will have to line the inside with cammo net or scrim, otherwise sunlight will be able to pass through the branches and reveal your shape. Test the bush for size and when you are satisfied, gather together all the cuttings, select a few bits and tie them together to make a door. The rest of the cuttings you will dispose of away from the site. Leave an object in the hide and fit your door. Now go off somewhere to get rid of the cuttings and have a kip. The next day you should go back to the bush and see if the object you placed inside is visible. If not, you have a viable site. Make sure that sunlight will not reflect off your camera or binocular lenses. Do not underestimate just how cold it gets when you are static, particularly at night. As you will be lying down, the greatest heat loss will be into the ground so insulate yourself from the earth with a kip mat. If the site is ever found you will almost certainly have left DNA evidence there. You can minimise this by tightly covering your hair, so that chunks of it are not ripped out by the bush, and by wearing thick clothes (knee pads, gloves, etc.), so that you don't leave blood on the thorns that are just dying to pierce your flesh. It is easy to leave stuff behind, particularly if you are leaving the site at night, so make sure that everything is in pockets, pouches or bumbag, and make sure that the pockets and other fastenings are done up securely.

CODE WORDS
Each group should have code words for use during exfiltration (leaving the area). For example, one code word may mean that the group is at its pickup point. Another may mean that both the primary and alternate pickup points are compromised and to forget about the pick up.

LOST COMMS

> "It's always useful to know where a friend-and-relation is, whether you want him or whether you don't." (Pooh's Little Instruction Book – Winnie the Pooh)

When a group has missed a certain number of required communications (set during the planning phase), the members of the group who have not taken part in the action assumes that the group has a communication problem, is in trouble, or both. At that time, the no-communication and exfiltration plan (also determined at the planning stage) is put into action.

Escape and Evasion

> "He who has a why to live for can bear almost any how." (Friedrich Nietzsche)

Getting away from the police and then staying out of their reach is what this section is all about. Escape is breaking away from the cops when surrounded. Evasion is eluding the cops during or after an action. Together, escape and evasion refer to the act of returning to safety by foot, essentially escaping from the cops and evading them to reach home.

> "The warrior: silent in his struggle, undetainable because he has nothing to lose, functional and efficacious because he has everything to gain." (Carlos Castaneda)

If you have been doing your training properly you will have been introducing increasingly greater levels of stress. And stress or state management techniques (or copious amounts of luck) are what you are going to need to bring into play if you are to be successful in an Escape and Evasion (E&E) situation. Although speed is of the essence in the initial stages of E&E, you must take that vital second to bring your panic under control enough to put together a rough plan, rather than just running blindly into the arms of more cops or up a dead-end street.

> "I'm not saying there won't be an Accident now, mind you. They're funny things, Accidents. You never have them till you're having them." (Winnie the Pooh)

The possibility of being sussed must always be considered, so you should plan for it in your planning phase and if E&E is a non-starter, you should measure the consequences of getting busted for a particular action against the worth of the action itself. First the group should check all factors that deal with evasion opportunities. Then you devise an evasion and escape plan. All members of the group must be completely clear about the evasion and escape plan. Each action has its own peculiar problems associated with evasion and escape and your plan should reflect this, while exploiting the individual capabilities and training of the group members. The group may be required to hide for several days to allow the police/security to become complacent before trying to move (see Survival section).

SHORT- AND LONG-RANGE E&E

"If there's trouble, all us freaks have is each other." (Abe Sapien – Hellboy)

In short-range evasion you, the evader, will usually have the means to return to safety within a few hours or maybe overnight. Long-range evasion involves greater distances where you may have to travel miles over unfamiliar terrain, possibly with little food and equipment. There are characteristics of successful long-range evasions that include: being able to cover great distances (see Fitness section), knowing survival techniques, conserving supplies, having a strong will to survive, having a sense of responsibility (the strong help the weak), panic control, continuous planning, patience, endurance, self-preservation, and knowledge of survival and evasion. At times it will almost certainly be impossible to travel without coming into contact with members of the public who may have heard that the cops are after someone, and you may need to use deception techniques, basically lying, using disguises and having a pretty good cover story. Deception is perhaps the most difficult type of evasion to take.

"War is an ugly thing, but not the ugliest of things. The decayed and degraded state of moral and patriotic feeling which thinks that nothing is worth war is much worse. The person who has nothing for which he is willing to fight, nothing which is more important than his own personal safety, is a miserable creature and has no chance of being free unless made and kept so by the exertions of better men than himself." (John Stewart Mill – didn't expect to see J.S. Mill did ya?)

HOW TO E&E SUCCESSFULLY
The following basic principles will go towards making the group successful at evasion. Number one, as always, is to have a detailed action plan which includes how to evade the police/security. Don't panic, take whatever time is needed, conserve your food and strength, rest and sleep when needed, survive, and return home.

If you become isolated you must find a safe hiding place where you can make an estimate of the situation and plan a course of action. Your plan should consider the following:

TRAVEL
Travel is critical for the evader because the chances of capture are greater while on the move. So try to avoid major roads and populated areas. Always use appropriate camouflage and concealment techniques and use a disguise as much

as possible if there is any chance of being spotted. When possible, travel during the hours of darkness, unless the police/security or possible witnesses know your location, in which case you must move immediately. Life will be much easier if the ground you are E&Eing over at night is terrain that you have been able to observe during the day. Time looking at the map, if you still have one, is never wasted. From it you may be able to work out routes that will give you the most concealment. The map should also help you spot possible obstacles on your route, which will give you time to work out how you are going to get past them. You may also be able to identify places along your route where you can lie up during the day.

After the initial escape, speed and distance are secondary to a safe route out of trouble.

Keep revising and updating your plan, but do not let your failure to meet a precise schedule inhibit the use of your plan.

OBSTACLES

Obstacles, which with any luck you have been able to identify from the map, will influence the selection of your routes. You may decide that deliberately crossing obstacles (see sections on Crossing Barriers and Defeating Security) will confuse your pursuers. You can split obstacles into two categories: natural and man-made. Natural obstacles are rivers, streams, mountains, etc., and man-made obstacles include electric fences and other barriers. It is obviously at the man-made obstacles you are most likely to encounter people.

"It is awfully hard to be b-b-brave, when you're only a Very Small Animal."
(Winnie the Pooh)

Urban Escape and Evasion

"A warrior is a hunter. He calculates everything. That's control. Once his calculations are over, he acts. He lets go. That's abandon. A warrior is not a leaf at the mercy of the wind. No one can push him; no one can make him do things against himself or against his better judgment. A warrior is tuned to survive, and he survives in the best of all possible fashions." (Carlos Castaneda)

DOWN TOWN
In many ways E&E is easier in town than in the country, certainly in the short term. Most of you reading this will be urbanites and even though you will probably have acted on the maxim that you do not shit in your own nest, i.e. you will not be doing the action in your own town, you will probably experience a generic familiarity in any town, which might give you some comfort.

PARANOID
It is highly unlikely that the state will be able to bring to bear against you many of the measures detailed below. You will find this thought reiterated in succeeding chapters because you need to keep things in perspective. But you also need to be switched on, aware, prepared and confident that you have, lodged firmly somewhere in your subconscious, the skills, tactics and techniques necessary to counter anything that comes your way.

JEEPERS, PEEPERS
CCTV is largely irrelevant in the first few crucial minutes of E&E. Although CCTV footage may be examined later, it is unlikely that the cops would be able to coordinate contemporaneous use of the cameras to aid them. Almost all the other detection methods (more on these later) can be defeated in a large town by the town itself, because of its clutter and interference. Even helicopter surveillance devices are useless if you stay under cover.

SOUNDS OF THE CITY
The physical characteristics of a town can actually aid your efforts at camouflage and concealment. The dense physical structure of urban areas generates clutter (an abundance of Electro Magnetic (EM) signatures in a given area). These signals are given off by just about every piece of electrical equipment, from the most sophisticated super computer down to the humble toaster and everything in between. This clutter increases the difficulty of identifying specific targets such as your escaping group. Urban clutter greatly reduces the effectiveness of police

surveillance sensors, particularly in the Infrared (IR) and radar wavelengths (see Appendix ii for more detailed information). This clutter generally makes visual cues the most important consideration in urban CC. The city provides an excellent background for concealing yourself and your kit. The regular pattern of urban terrain, the diverse colours and contrast and the large, enclosed structures offer a variety of concealment opportunities. Road surfaces effectively mask vehicle tracks: you are not leaving muddy tracks cross country and, depending on the nature of the action, numerous members of the general public and their vehicles could be present and may well serve as cover. This confuses the cops' ability to distinguish between activist targets and shoppers or club goers.

Underground structures (sewers, etc.) are excellent means of concealing movement (but rather smelly). Note that these systems are always sealed when something high profile is going on – Party conference, G8 meeting, etc. When augmented by artificial means, man-made structures provide symmetrical shapes that provide ready-made CC. You must limit or conceal movement and shine (see Camouflage section) as these provide the best opportunities for you to be spotted in town. Obviously where you place your equipment, vehicles and people remains important to provide visual CC and to avoid detection by contrast (thermal sensors detecting people and equipment silhouetted against colder buildings or other large, flat surfaces). The fundamental CC rule is, as always, to maintain the natural look of an area as much as possible.

Buildings with large, thick walls and a few narrow windows provide the best concealment. It is very unlikely that these huge police resources will be used against you while you are in the recce/surveillance phase unless your group has been compromised and is being watched anyway but it is worth taking the added precautions. And these precautions should certainly be used if you are on the run.

URBAN TERRAIN
Urbanisation is reducing the amount of open, natural terrain throughout the world. Our government is certainly making sure that in the UK any green bits that haven't been chopped down and tarmacked over to service the movement of the internal combustion engine will be suffocated under unaffordable houses and football stadia. As a consequence, your group must be able to apply effective urban Camouflage and Concealment. Many of the CC techniques used in natural terrain (see Camouflage section) are effective in urban areas.

ANGLES AND DISTANCE

If an action goes tits up and you have to E&E in town, the first consideration is to put as great a distance as possible between your-selves and the forces of law and order, but this should be done tactically. If you run in a straight line, e.g. following the same road, you will become an easy target: either you will be intercepted (the cops radio another unit) or a vehicle comes after you. So the first thing you need to do is throw in lots of angles, e.g. take a left turn down the first road you get to, then a right (you don't want to do a full 360°) and keep doing the same sort of thing – if you have done a thorough recce of the area you won't end up going down a dead-end street or past the cop shop. If the initial E&E has been done as a group, you should split up as soon as possible. Crossroads are great as the cops have to split their forces to cover all the possible directions. Get far away from the scene of the action as quickly as possible. In all situations where you are doing E&E the importance of angles and distance cannot be over emphasised.

SPEND, SPEND, SPEND

There is always the possibility that you will have to really get away, possibly even leaving the country, and this is where biometric data on passports could be a problem. Try and get good false ID. It is worth having lots and lots of credit cards, so start opening your junk mail. If you have, say, 20 credit cards you could get at least £5,000 per day from the hole in the wall and spend about £120,000 on easily converted items and maybe, as a one off, a travel ticket. Remember of course that all transactions can be tracked so you could not use the cards for very many transactions, maybe even just once. But they are certainly a useful resource.

Tracking and Counter-Tracking

"Good walking leaves no track behind it." (*Tao Te Ching* – Lao Tsu)

Tracking (what they do) and counter-tracking (how you avoid being nicked) are techniques worth having a brief look at. This level of response is only likely if the action has been a really, really serious one and the group has had to do a runner across country, but at least a working knowledge of this stuff might come in handy one of these days.

CONCEPTS OF TRACKING

To become a good tracker a person probably needs some sort of innate aptitude but there are certain essential qualities that can be developed and refined such as patience, persistence, acute observation, good memory, and intuition. These traits help when the tracking signs become weak or if the tracker has a certain feeling about the situation. As the tracker moves, they will form an opinion about what (who) they are tracking, such as how many there are, how well trained they are, the equipment they have, and state of their morale, etc. The following six indicators help form the tracker's picture of the quarry (possibly you).

DISPLACEMENT

Displacement means that something has been moved from its original position. The tracker looks for signs of displacement for 10 to 15 metres in a 180-degree arc to his/her front from the ground to the average height of a person. By comparing indicators, the tracker can gain information. A footprint can tell the tracker what footgear the person is wearing, if any. It can also show the lack of proper equipment, the direction of movement, number of persons, whether they are carrying heavy loads, the sex, rate of movement, and whether or not they know they are being followed. Other forms of displacement are bits of clothing or thread left on the ground or vegetation. Movement of vegetation on a still day (such as broken limbs and bent grass, animals flushed from their homes or cries of excitement, paths cut through foliage, disturbed insect life, or turned over rocks) indicates a presence.

STAINING

A good example of staining is blood on the ground or foliage. Other examples of staining are mud dragged by footgear and crushed vegetation on a hard object. Crushed berries also stain. The movement of water causes it to become cloudy.

WEATHERING
The weather may help or hinder the tracker to determine the age of signs. Wind, snow, rain and sunlight are factors affecting tracking signs.

LITTERING
A poorly disciplined group will pass through an area leaving a path of litter. A tracker can use the last rain or strong wind as a measure to show the amount of time it has been there.

CAMOUFLAGING TECHNIQUES
Camouflage applies to tracking when the followed group or individual tries to slow down the tracker. For example, leaving footprints walking backward, brushing out paths, and walking over rocky ground or through streams are ways of camouflaging the path.

YOU AIN'T NOTHING BUT A HOUND DOG
Tracker and dog groups are more effective than a tracker alone. The dog(s) follows a path faster and can continue to track at night. Despite years of domestication, dogs retain most of the traits of their wild ancestors. If put to a controlled use by their handler, these traits are effective when tracking. Dogs exhibit great endurance. A dog can hold a steady pace and effectively track for up to eight hours. The speed can be up to 10 miles per hour, only limited by the speed of the handler. Their speed and endurance can be further increased by the use of vehicles and extra groups. Dogs are curious by nature. They can be aggressive or lazy, cowardly or brave. It is the dog's sensory traits which make it seem intelligent. Tracking dogs are screened and trained. They are aggressive trackers and eager to please their handler.

What You Need To Know
Knowledge of the following sensory traits and how the dog uses them could help you to think ahead of the dog.

Sight
A dog's vision is the lesser of its sensing abilities. They see in black and white and have difficulty spotting static objects at more than 50 yards. Dogs can spot moving objects at considerable distances. However, they do not look up unless they have been trained to look up a tree. A dog's night vision is no better than a person's.

Hearing
A dangerous problem for the evader is the dog's ability to hear. Dogs can hear quieter and higher frequencies than humans. Even more dangerous is their ability to locate the source of the sound. Dogs can hear 40 times better than people.

Smell
The dog's sense of smell is about 900 times better than a human's. It is by far its greatest asset and the largest threat to the evader. Dogs can detect minute signs of disturbance on the ground or even in the air. Using distracting or irritating odours (for example, CS powder or pepper) only bothers the dog for a short time (3 to 5 minutes). After the odour is discharged by the dog, it can pick-up a cold path even quicker. The dog smells odours from the ground and air and forms scent pictures. The scent pictures are put together through several sources of smell.

Individual Scent
This is the most important scent when it comes to tracking. Vapours from body secretions work their way through the evader's shoes onto the ground. Sweat from other parts of the body rubs off onto vegetation and other objects. Scent is even left in the air.

Reinforcing Scent
Objects are introduced to the dog that reinforces the scent as it relates to the evader. Some reinforcing scents could be on the evader's clothing or boots, or the same material as is used in his/her clothing. Even boot polish can help the dog.

Ecological Scent
For the dog, the most important scent comes from the earth itself. By far, the strongest smells come from disturbances in ecology such as crushed insects, bruised vegetation and broken ground. Over varied terrain, dogs can smell particles and vapours that are constantly carried by the evader wherever they walk.

Favourable Tracking Conditions
Seldom will the conditions be ideal for the tracker and dog groups. During training, they become familiar with the difficulties they will face and learn to deal with them. The following conditions are favourable for tracker and dog groups:
- **Fresh scent**: This is probably the most important factor for tracker groups. The fresher the scent, the greater the chances of success.
- **Verified starting point**: If trackers have a definite scent to introduce to the dogs, it helps the dogs to follow the correct path.
- **Unclean evader**: An unclean evader leaves a more distinctive scent.

- **Fast-moving evader**: A fast-moving evader causes more ground disturbances and individual scent from sweat.
- **Night and early morning**: The air is thicker and the scent lasts longer.
- **Cool, cloudy weather**: This limits evaporation of scent.
- **No wind**: This keeps the scent close to the ground. It also keeps it from spreading around, allowing the dog to follow the correct route.
- **Thick vegetation**: This restricts the dissemination of scent and holds the smell.

Unfavourable Tracking Conditions
Marked loss in technique proficiency can be expected when the following conditions occur:
- **Heat**: This causes rapid evaporation of scent.
- **Unverified start point**: The dogs may follow the wrong route or scent.
- **Low humidity**: Scent does not last as long.
- **Dry ground**: Dry ground does not retain scent.
- **Wind**: Wind disperses scent and causes the dog to track downwind.
- **Heavy rain**: This washes the scent away.

Distractive scents
These take the dog's attention away from the path. Some of these scents are blood, meat, manure, farmland and populated areas.

Covered Scent, Hug a Cow
Some elements in nature cause the scent picture to be partially or completely covered. Examples are sand that can blow over the tracks and help to disguise the track; snow and ice that can form over the track and make it nearly impossible to follow; and water. Water is one of the most difficult conditions for a tracker dog group. Water that is shallow, especially if rocks or vegetation protrude, can produce a path that a dog can follow with varied degrees of success. If appropriate, you could cross a field where cattle or sheep are grazing to confuse your scent.

COUNTER-TRACKING
Counter-tracking techniques are used to avoid alerting the police to your presence. To be effective at evading trackers you need to know a few counter tracking techniques. Knowing how trackers and tracker and dog groups go about their job is probably the best way to successfully evade trackers (see above) and will greatly assist you if you have to evade the police and possibly army (depends how bad they want you). Some of the following techniques may throw off trackers:

- **Double back**: Especially when moving into open areas.
- **Use paths**: Follow or pretend to follow, then double back.
- **Walk backwards**: This makes the tracker believe the evader is moving in the opposite direction.
- **Change directions** before entering streams.
- **Walk in water**

Cover the path. Outdistance trackers. Take advantage of terrain and weather conditions; for example, use streams and sparsely vegetated areas to move through, and move during heavy rains. Work needs to be done on counter-tracking techniques, but I think the bottom line is that the dog is always attached to its handler and therefore can only move as fast as the handler. The trick is to wear out the handler. If you are moving through lots of undergrowth you leave lots of signs, but you also provide lots of opportunity for tangled leads. Get the handler to distrust their dog by moving in strange ways – zig-zagging or covering the same piece of ground several times or crossing and re-crossing rivers.

How They May Find Us

The state can call upon a huge array of tracking technology. Whether they use it against you will depend on how much of a threat they perceive you to be or how much political capital they can make out of capturing you. Anyway I found these two items on the Ministry of Defence (MoD) website.

Man-portable Surveillance and Target Acquisition Radar (MSTAR)

MSTAR is a lightweight, all-weather battlefield radar, able to detect helicopters, vehicles and infantry (or your group) to a range in excess of 20km. The electro-luminescent display shows dead ground, relief and target track history, and a 1:50,000 map grid can be superimposed to simplify the transfer of information to and from military maps. The 30kg radar can be carried in a vehicle or broken down into three easily man-packed loads.

Intelligence, Surveillance, Target Acquisition and Reconnaissance Equipment (ISTAR)

ISTAR equipment includes image-intensifying goggles, lightweight thermal imagers and laser target markers. Thermal imaging (TI) turns heat into light – allowing the user to see through darkness, rain or undergrowth. Body heat makes people appear bright: vehicles are visible by the heat from their engines – or even from warm tyres. LION is a lightweight thermal imager used at platoon level to detect targets at medium range, while Sophie is a long-range system deployed at company level. TADS is a thermal imaging sight that can be fitted to the long-range L96 Sniper Rifle used by sniper teams. Larger and more powerful thermal imagers are Spyglass and OTIS, which are used by artillery observers and is normally mounted on the Warrior Observation Post Vehicle.

THE TECHNOLOGY BIT

The next section will look at some of the toys you taxpayers have been buying for the boys and girls in blue and green and how we can defeat them.

Near Infra Red Sensors (NIR)

The closest to visible light, near-IR has wavelengths that range from 0.7 to 1.3 microns, or 700 billionths to 1,300 billionths of a metre. (See Appendix ii) While red filters help preserve night vision, they cannot prevent NIR from detecting light from long distances. Therefore, careful light discipline is an important counter-measure to NIR sensors and visual sensors (such as image intensifiers).

Mid-infrared (Mid-IR)

Mid-IR has wavelengths ranging from 1.3 to 3 microns. Both near-IR and mid-IR are used by a variety of electronic devices, including remote controls.

Thermal-infrared (Thermal-IR)

Occupying the largest part of the infrared spectrum, thermal-IR has wavelengths ranging from 3 microns to over 30 microns.

Infra Red Sensors (IR)

Natural materials and terrain shield heat sources from IR sensors and break up the shape of cold and warm targets viewed on IR sensors. Don't lift up your vehicle's bonnet in an attempt to break windshield glare because this just exposes a hot spot for IR detection – cover the windshield with a basha or spare clothing. Even if the IR system is capable of locating a target, the target's actual identity can still be disguised. Avoid building unnecessary fires. Use vehicle heaters only when necessary. (See Appendix ii)

The key difference between thermal-IR and the other two is that thermal-IR is emitted by an object instead of reflected off it. Infrared light is emitted by an object because of what is happening at the atomic level.

Ultraviolet Sensors (UV)

These sensors are a significant threat in snow-covered areas. Winter camo paint and terrain masking can help you beat this type of sensor. Any kind of smoke will defeat UV sensors. Field-expedient countermeasures, such as constructing snow walls also provide a means of defeating UV sensors. (See Appendix ii)

Radar

Police use MTI (see below), imaging and radar.

Moving Target Indicator (MTI)

This radar is a threat. Where possible don't use metal – most radar can detect these items. Movement discipline is very important. Moving by covered routes (terrain masking) prevents radar detection. Slow, deliberate movements across areas exposed to radar coverage helps avoid detection by MTI radar. Flattening yourself against a wall and moving slowly may also help.

Vehicles are large radar-reflecting targets, and a skilled MTI operator can even identify the type of vehicle. Moving vehicles can be detected by MTI radar from 20 kilometres, but travelling by covered routes helps protect against surveillance.

Imaging

Imaging radar is not a threat to individuals and concealing vehicles behind earth, masonry walls or dense foliage effectively screens them. Light foliage may provide complete visual concealment, however, it is sometimes totally transparent to imaging radar.

Acoustic Sensors

Being serious about noise discipline should stop you being heard by a human ear. And you can try to confuse electronic measures with fireworks or use Iron Maiden (Ride of the Valkyries?) played very loudly to screen your noise, cover inherently noisy activities, and confuse sound interpretation. Stage a street party, maybe.

Radio Sensors

The best way to prevent the police from locating radio transmitters is to minimise transactions. Pre-planning message traffic, transmitting as quickly as possible, and using alternate communication means whenever possible will reduce the chances of you being overheard and deffed (direction found). To prevent the police/security from intercepting radio communications, change the radio frequencies, and use terrain masking.

The Vehicle Question

The next section looks at the added problems associated with trying to use vehicles to get the group and kit to surveillance sites or the target itself. It is unlikely, certainly in the short term, that you will be mounting an action that requires this level of consideration but better safe than sorry.

If you get bumped during or on the way to surveillance the consequences are not going to be huge, the main thing is that you are going to have to bin that particular action. Having a completely legal vehicle in this instance is really important (although if you are captured by CCTV or twigged by security and your licence plates noted, you could be in trouble if the subsequent action is traced back to you).

Vehicles left overnight just about anywhere will attract attention so if surveillance is going to take several hours, overnight or multi-day, make sure your vehicle is hidden or innocuous.

For the action itself, which should not take too long, if you really need a vehicle(s) consider stealing it/them. Perhaps it will be decided at the planning stage that the action will have a greater chance of success if there are several vehicles parked up along the escape route and you change from one to the other. You could change the appearance of the vehicle(s) by painting, changing licence plates or covering them with mud (make sure that the rest of the vehicle is mud spattered as well). Don't steal the car immediately before the action – you need to have the time to check it over and make sure it won't conk out on you. Steal anonymous cars (common make and unremarkable colour). A mini-bus will stand out more than several cars.

MINIMISING MOVEMENT

As noted several times previously, your movement attracts attention and this is obviously even more pronounced when you have wheels that also produce a number of signatures (tracks, noise, hot spots and dust). On actions that involve you charging around in a vehicle, plan discipline and manage movement so that signatures are reduced as much as possible. Movement against a stationary background really stands out. Remember that regular movement is usually less obvious than fast, erratic movement.

REFLECTANCE

Reflectance is the amount of energy returned from a target's surface as compared to the energy striking the surface. Reflectance is generally described in terms of the part of the EM spectrum in which the reflection occurs. Visual reflectance is characterised by the colour of a target. Colour contrast can be important, particularly at close ranges and in homogeneous background environments such as snow or desert terrain. The longer the range, the less important colour becomes.

At very long ranges, all colours tend to merge into a uniform tone. Also, the human eye cannot discriminate colour in poor light. Temperature reflectance is the thermal energy reflected by a target (except when the thermal energy of a target is self-generated, as in the case of a hot engine). IR imaging sensors measure and detect differences in temperature-reflectance levels (known as thermal contrast). Radar-signal reflectance is the part of the incoming radio waves that is reflected by a target. Radar sensors detect differences in a target's reflected radar return and that of the background. Since metal is an efficient radio-wave reflector and vehicles are made of metals, radar return is an important reflectance factor. Try to bear all these things in mind and work out ways in which to disguise all the signs of your presence. Here are some suggestions.

TRACKS
Vehicle tracks are clearly visible from the air, particularly in selected terrain. Therefore, track and movement discipline is essential. Use existing roads and tracks as much as possible. When using new paths, ensure that they fit into the existing terrain's pattern. Minimise, plan, and coordinate all movement; take full advantage of cover and dead space.

HIDING
Hiding means screening yourself from police sensors. You can't be detected if a barrier hides you from a sensor's view. Every effort should be made to hide all operations; this includes using conditions of limited visibility for movement and terrain masking. Examples of hiding include: placing vehicles beneath tree canopies; placing equipment in defilade positions; covering vehicles and equipment with nets.

BLENDING
Blending is trying to alter your appearance so that you become a part of the background. Generally, it is arranging or applying camouflage material on, over, and/or around to reduce your contrast with the background. Characteristics to consider when blending include the terrain patterns in the vicinity and the size, shape, texture, colour of yourself and/or vehicle, EM signature, and background.

SHAPE
Nature is pretty random, while most equipment has regular features with hard, angular lines – even an erected camouflage net takes on a shape with straight-line edges or smooth curves between support points. So arrange camouflage accordingly. Remember sensors can detect targets against any background unless their shape is disguised or disrupted.

SIZE
Size, which is implicitly related to shape, can also distinguish a target from its background. So again disguise the size to make your vehicle fit in with the shape of the landscape.

CAMO PAINT
Camo painted vehicles blend well with the background and can hide from optical sensors better than those painted a solid, subdued colour. But you are going to stick out if you try to drive down the street painted like a tree, so if you intend going for the camo paint option only paint up when you are in position and make sure you use paint that you can wash off quickly. Pattern-painted equipment enhances anti-detection by reducing shape, shadow, and colour signatures. It is very unlikely that you will be able to get your hands on 'improved paint' down B&Q, which is a shame as, like the dyes in camo clothing, it can stop you being detected in the visible and IR portions of the EM spectrum. The result is a vehicle or an item of equipment that blends better with its background when viewed by police sensors.

CAMOUFLAGE NETS
A new camouflage net reduces a vehicle's visual and radar signatures. Stainless steel fibres in the material absorb some of the radar signal and reflect most of the remaining signal in all directions. The result is a small percentage of signal return to the radar for detection. The radar-scattering capabilities of the net are effective only if there is at least 2 feet of space between it and the camouflaged equipment and if it completely covers the equipment.

VEGETATION
You can use branches and vines to temporarily conceal vehicles, equipment and people. Attach the vegetation to equipment with plastic cable ties, bits of string, etc. Use other foliage to complete the camouflage or to supplement natural-growing vegetation. You can also use cut foliage to augment other artificial CC materials, such as branches placed on a camouflage net to break up its outline. Be careful when placing green vegetation since the underside of leaves presents a lighter tone in photographs. Replace cut foliage often because it wilts and changes colour rapidly. During training exercises, ensure that cutting vegetation and foliage does not adversely effect the natural environment.

LIVING VEGETATION
Just because you are on a mission doesn't mean that you can be an environmental vandal. If you need to cut living branches be selective and make sure that you are

not going to cause any permanent damage to the tree. Living vegetation can be obtained in most environments, and its colour and texture make it a good blending agent. However, foliage requires careful maintenance to keep the material fresh and in good condition. If branches are not placed in their proper growing positions, they may reveal positions to police or security observers. Cutting large amounts of branches can also reveal positions, so cut all vegetation away from the target areas. Living vegetation presents a chlorophyll response at certain NIR wavelengths. As cut vegetation wilts, it loses colour and its NIR-blending properties, which are related to the chlorophyll response. Replace cut vegetation regularly because over time it becomes a detection cue rather than an effective concealment technique.

SHADOW
Shadow can be divided into two types. A cast shadow is a silhouette of an object projected against its background. It is the more familiar type and can be highly conspicuous. In desert environments, a shadow cast by a target can be more conspicuous than the target itself. A contained shadow is the dark pool that forms in a permanently shaded area (e.g. under a vehicle). Contained shadows show up much darker than their surroundings and are easily detected. As above, disguising the shape will make the shadow seem innocuous.

NOISE
Noise and acoustic signatures produced by activities and equipment are recognisable. So you should try to avoid or minimise actions that produce noise. Communications people should operate their equipment at the lowest possible level that allows them to be heard and understood. Depending on the terrain and atmospheric conditions, noise can travel great distances and reveal the group's position.

TEXTURE
A rough surface appears darker than a smooth surface, even if both surfaces are the same colour. For example, vehicle tracks change the texture of the ground by

 leaving clearly visible track marks. This is particularly true in undisturbed or homogeneous environments, such as a desert or virgin snow, where vehicle tracks are highly detectable. In extreme cases, the texture of glass or other very smooth surfaces causes a shine that acts as a beacon. Under normal conditions, very smooth surfaces stand out from the background. Therefore, eliminating shine must be a high priority.

PATTERNS

The camo patterns on any vehicle or the kit you are carrying often differ considerably from background patterns. The critical relationships that determine the contrast between a piece of equipment and its background are the distance between the observer and the equipment and the distance between the equipment and its background. Since these distances usually vary, it is difficult to paint equipment with a pattern that always allows it to blend with its background. As such, no single pattern is prescribed for all situations. Field observations provide the best match between equipment and background. The overall terrain pattern and the signatures produced by activity on the terrain are important recognition factors. If a group's presence is to remain unnoticed, it must match the signatures produced by stationary equipment, vehicles and other activities with the terrain pattern. Careful attention must also be given to vehicle tracks and their affect on the local terrain as you move into and out of a site.

SITE SELECTION

This is extremely important because your location and that of your equipment can eliminate or reduce recognition factors. If a vehicle is positioned so that it faces probable sensor locations, the thermal signature from its hot engine compartment is minimised. If a vehicle is positioned under foliage, the exhaust will disperse and cool as it rises, reducing its thermal signature and blending it more closely with the background. Placing equipment in defilade (dug-in) positions prevents detection by ground-mounted radar. The following factors should govern site selection:

THE ACTION

The action is the most important factor in site selection. A particular site may be excellent from a CC standpoint, but the site is useful only if the action is accomplished. If a site is so obvious that the police will find it before the action has happened, the site was poorly selected to begin with. Not getting nicked is usually a part of most actions, so groups must first evaluate the worthiness of a site with respect to action accomplishment and then consider camo.

TERRAIN PATTERNS

Every type of terrain, even a flat desert, has a discernible pattern. Terrain features can blur or conceal the signatures of activity. By using terrain features, CC effectiveness can be enhanced without relying on additional materials. The primary factor to consider is whether using the site will disturb the terrain pattern enough to attract the attention of the police or any security that the target has. The goal is not to disturb the terrain pattern at all. Any change in an existing terrain pattern will indicate the presence of activity. Terrain patterns have distinctive characteristics that you need to preserve. The three general terrain patterns that concern us are:

- **Agricultural** terrain has a chessboard or patchwork pattern when viewed from aircraft. This is a result of the different types of crops and vegetation found on most farms.
- **Urban** terrain is characterised by uniform rows of housing with interwoven streets and interspersed trees and shrubs.
- **Woodlands** are characterised by natural, irregular features (except plantations), unlike the geometric patterns of agricultural and urban terrains. Forests generally provide the best type of natural screen against optical recce, especially if the crowns of the trees are wide enough to prevent aerial observation of the ground. Forests with undergrowth also hinder ground observation. Deciduous forests are not as effective during the months when trees are bare, while coniferous forests preserve their concealment properties all year. When possible, group movements should be made along roads and gaps that are covered by tree crowns. Shade should be used to conceal vehicles, equipment, and people from aerial observation. Limited visibility is an especially important concealment tool when conducting operations in open terrain. The police, however, will conduct searches with a combination of night-surveillance devices, radar, IR sensors, and terrain illumination.

CC DISCIPLINE

CC discipline is avoiding an activity that changes the appearance of an area or reveals the presence of your equipment. CC discipline is a continuous necessity that applies to everyone. If you screw up any of the visual and audio routines the entire CC effort may fail. Vehicle tracks, spoil and debris are the most common signs of activity and their presence can negate all your efforts of proper placement and concealment. CC discipline should prevent the police/security from observing any of the indications of your location or activities by minimizing disturbances to a target area. To help maintain group viability, a group must integrate all available CC means into a cohesive plan. CC discipline involves regulating light, heat, noise, spoil, rubbish and movement. Successful CC discipline depends largely on the actions of individual people. Some of these actions may not be easy on you but your failure to observe CC discipline could defeat the entire group's CC efforts and possibly cause the group's action to fail and arrests to happen.

A Bit More Discipline

Do lots of CC practice. Light and heat discipline, though important at all times, are crucial at night. As long as visual observation remains a primary recce method, concealing light signatures remains an important CC countermeasure. Lights that are not blacked out at night can be observed at great distances. For example, the human eye can detect camp fires from 8 kilometres and vehicle lights from 20 kilometres. When using heat sources is unavoidable, use terrain masking, exhaust baffling, and other techniques to minimise thermal signatures of fires and stoves.

Get Rid Of Your Crap
The prompt and complete disposal of debris and spoil is an essential CC consideration. Proper spoil discipline removes a key signature of a group's current or past presence in an area.

Dead Ground
Groups should not locate or move along the topographic crests of hills or other locations where they are silhouetted against the sky. They should use reverse slopes of hills, ravines, embankments and other terrain features as screens to avoid detection by ground-mounted sensors. Use the line-of-sight (LOS) method to identify areas of dead ground.

DATA SOURCES
You need to be able to evaluate natural conditions in the area to effectively direct group concealment. You must know the terrain and weather conditions before going on the action. In addition to weather reports (internet, radio, etc.) and maps, you should use aerial photographs, recce and information gathered from locals to determine the terrain's natural concealment properties.

A DRIED FLOWER ARRANGEMENT
Use dead vegetation (dried grass, hay, straw, branches) for texturing. It provides good blending qualities if the surrounding background vegetation is also dead. Dead vegetation is usually readily available and requires little maintenance; however, it is flammable. Due to the absence of chlorophyll response, dead vegetation offers little CC against NIR sensors and hyperspectral sensors operating in the IR regions.

A BOUQUET OF BRACKEN
When you are out picking your vegetation consider the following:
• Coniferous vegetation is more useful than deciduous vegetation since it maintains a valid chlorophyll response longer after being cut.
• Foliage cut during periods of high humidity (at night, during a rainstorm, or when there is fog or heavy dew) will wilt more slowly.
• Foliage with leaves that feel tough to the fingers and branches with large leaves are preferred because they stay fresher longer.
• Branches that grow in direct sunlight are tougher and will stay fresher longer.
• Branches that are free of disease and insects will not wilt as rapidly.

CHLOROPHYLL RESPONSE

Standard camouflage materials are designed to exhibit an artificial chlorophyll response at selected NIR wavelengths. Non-standard materials (sheets, tarps) are not likely to exhibit a chlorophyll response and will not blend well with standard CC material or natural vegetation. Use non-standard materials only as CC treatments against visual threat sensors, not against NIR or hyperspectral threat sensors.

MUD, GLORIOUS MUD

With expedient paint, basically we are talking about throwing mud over your vehicle and equipment. You can use earth, sand, and gravel to change or add colour, provide a coarse texture and create shapes and shadows. Mud is excellent for toning down bright, shiny objects (glass, tools, watches). You can also add clay (in mud form) of various colours to crankcase oil to produce a field-expedient paint. This table below should give you a few ideas of how to mix soil-based expedient paints. Try and use surface soils to mimic the natural surface colour and reflectivity.

Paint Materials	Mixing	Colour	Finish
Earth, soap, water, soot, paraffin	Mix soot with paraffin, add to solution of 8 gal water and 2 bars soap, and stir in earth	Dark grey	Flat, lustreless
Oil, clay, water, petrol, earth	Mix 2 gal water with 1 gal oil and to gal clay, add earth, and thin with petrol or water	Depends on earth colours	Glossy on metal, otherwise dull
Oil, clay, soap, water, earth	Mix 1 bar soap with 3 gal water, add 1 gal oil, stir in 1 gal clay, and add earth for colour	Depends on earth colours	Glossy on metal, otherwise dull

Note: You can use canned milk or powdered eggs to increase the binding properties of field-expedient paints. (The vegan option is to use soya/gram flour.)

SPECIAL ENVIRONMENTS
The fundamentals of CC do not change between environments. However, the guidelines for their application change. Different environments require thoughtful, creative and unique CC techniques.

SNOW COVERED AREAS
When the main background is white, you can use whitewash over your permanent paint job. This will work well if the snow cover is more than 85 percent.

Placement
A blanket of snow often eliminates much of the ground pattern, causing natural textures and colours to disappear. Blending under these conditions is difficult. However, snow-covered terrain is rarely completely white so use the dark features of the landscape. Place equipment in roadways, in streambeds, under trees, under bushes, in shadows, and in ground folds.

Movement
Concealing tracks is a major problem in snow-covered environments. Movement should follow wind-swept drift lines, which cast shadows, as much as possible. Vehicle drivers should avoid sharp turns and follow existing track marks. Wipe out

short lengths of track marks by trampling them with snowshoes or by brushing them out.

Thermal Signatures

Snow-covered environments provide excellent conditions for their thermal and UV sensors. Terrain masking is the best solution to counter both types of sensors. Use arctic camo nets and winter camouflage paint to provide UV blending. (See Appendix ii)

PART SIX

AFTER THE PARTY

PLUS
AFTERMATH & APPENDICES

Part Six. This concluding section covers the inevitable 'what next?' and includes some useful appendices

Post-Action

Things will never be quite the same again. You will have learnt that you can do it, which will be tremendously important to you whatever the accompanying emotions are. Fear, elation, frustration and satisfaction in various degrees will be flooding through you. You will certainly be on a high and will have a clearer idea of what you are capable of. You might have discovered that you are not cut out for this sort of thing and that your first real action will be your last. More likely, however, is that you just want to get on with the next action as soon as possible. Over the following days and weeks your emotions will probably go up and down and will not necessarily be related or proportional to the effectiveness of the action itself.

DEBRIEF

However the action goes there are bound to be lessons to learn. Try and have a meeting as soon as possible after the action to discuss how the planning and execution of it went (and to celebrate). You should go through all the strengths and weaknesses of all the various stages of planning and carrying out the action. Think about what was good and bad and try and learn lessons for the next action. This is best done in the first few days, after the adrenaline has subsided but before memories get fuzzy and important details are forgotten.

MUTUAL AID

"A little Consideration, a little Thought for Others, makes all the difference." (Pooh's Little Instruction Book – Winnie the Pooh)

Look after yourself and one another. Don't pressure people to go on future actions if they are tired or stressed out. Take time out to relax and don't get into 'the struggle is my life' martyrdom headspace. Address problems and power relations within the group. In the longer term make an effort to learn skills that only one or two people have. This stops them being put under unnecessary pressure and ensures a balance of responsibility.

SECURITY

Don't let your security slacken because the action is in the past. Don't blab about the action; make sure you have not set any paper trails back to you; make sure there are no records of communications; make sure that any kit, equipment, disguises, etc. used on the action are cached somewhere safe or destroyed. The cops have long memories and if your action is considered serious by the state an investigation into it can continue for months – or even years.

THE NEXT STEP

"Tomorrow's battle is won during today's practice." (Samurai maxim)

Post-Action Training

A training plan should be devised to address the results of the after-action review. Training replacement group members may also be necessary.

   The importance of continued training cannot be over emphasised. Get out there with your mates and set each other navigational tasks. Make fools of yourselves by trying to move tactically, using CC, crawling and all the rest. Practice making observation points and building hides. Set up perimeter security to see how switched on everyone is. You can buy, legally, trip wire and pressure mines that use blank shotgun shells and flares. The use of flares is to be recommended to make everything seem more realistic. (Use white flares not red ones, unless you want to be rescued.) Smoke bombs are also useful for creating a confusing training environment. You can buy smoke and paintball grenades, military thunderflashes, stun grenades and screening smoke at www.outdoorsman.co.uk. Be effective, have fun, be safe.

> "The men of the future will yet fight their way to many a liberty that we do not even miss." (Max Stirner)

You have already made a difference

> "The flapping of a single butterfly's wing today produces a tiny change in the state of the atmosphere. Over a period of time, what the atmosphere actually does diverges from what it would have done. So, in a month's time, a tornado that would have devastated the Indonesian coast doesn't happen. Or maybe one that wasn't going to happen, does." (*Does God Play Dice? The Mathematics of Chaos* – Ian Stewart)

What you have just done may have been a discrete stand alone action, part of a campaign, an anonymous intervention (in an industrial dispute, for example), or part of a larger future action. Whatever it is, try not to ascribe value to the action itself by holding it alongside what you perceive to be the effect of the action. It is easy to feel emotionally flat after the adrenalin wears off and want to throw yourself into the next action, just for the sake of doing something – this can be dangerous. You may even feel depressed that, despite all the hard work you put into the action, nothing seems to have changed.

Harbouring negative thoughts about the effectiveness of your contribution to the struggle can be debilitating, and in the immediate aftermath of the action it is not possible to evaluate the ultimate or cumulative effect it will have or the inspiration it will give others. The application of Chaos theory to the sweep of political affairs would be an interesting field of study.

Who would have thought at the start of the 1980s that the prevailing political ideology of most of Europe would, overnight, pack its battered dialectical bags and slink off, stage right, to the sound of a crumbling wall.

Who could have predicted that, at the start of the last century, a single shot would be the catalyst which sent millions of young men to slaughter each other during the First World War. Or that a dogged adherence to the concept of the Poll Tax and the total failure to comprehend the lengths that people would go to not to pay it would sweep away the Iron Lady.

You have already changed the world. You are a butterfly wing – wrapped around a brick.

L. Hobley, Airstrip One, March 2006

> "My life is simple, my food is plain, and my quarters are uncluttered. In all things, I have sought clarity. I face the troubles and problems of life and death willingly. Virtue, integrity and courage are my priorities. I can be approached, but never pushed; befriended but never coerced; killed but never shamed." (Last letter to an old friend – Yi Sunshin)

Dedicated to the memory of Percy Toplis

Glossary

Actions On Scenarios to deal with events, dear boy

Acoustic Sensors From human ears to electronic listening devices

Affinity Group A group of like-minded individuals (not to be confused with a cadre)

Basha A camouflaged tarp – another name for a Hooch

BB(s) Small (6mm) spherical plastic projectiles used in Air Soft guns

Bivi To bivouac

Bivi bag A waterproof bivouac sac

Bivouac (1) Impromptu and/or uncomfortable sleeping arrangements.
(2) Sleeping outside sans tent.

BMC British Mountaineering Council

Bungee Elastic shock cord

Call Sign A clear way of identifying yourself during radio traffic which does not involve using your real name. And a ten four to you, good buddy.

CTR close target reconnaissance

CCTV Closed Circuit TeleVision

CPR Cardio Pulmonary Resuscitation

CS Tear gas or smoke

CC Camouflage and Concealment

Comms Communications – usually radio
   Lost Communications failure

Camo Camouflage

Defilade In a hole

Discipline
   Noise discipline muffles and eliminates sounds made by people and their equipment
   Movement discipline minimises movement
   Light discipline controls the use of lights at night

Dispersal The deliberate deployment of people and equipment over a wide area.

E&E Escape and Evasion

EM Electro Magnetic

Enfilade From the side

Entrenching tool Folding shovel

Exfiltration Getting out of an area

Expedient (field) Improvised

Gillie suit Camouflage clothing festooned with strips of Hessian to break up silhouette

GPS Global Positioning System

Hide Cover where you can see without being seen

Hooch An improvised shelter

IRR Infra Red Reflective

IR Infra Red

ISTAR Intelligence, Surveillance, Target Acquisition and Reconnaissance Equipment

Infiltration Getting into an area

LION A lightweight thermal imager

Line-of-sight (LOS) An imaginary straight line between observer and observed

L96 Sniper rifle used by sniper teams.

MoD Ministry of Defence

MSTAR Man-portable Surveillance and Target Acquisition Radar

MIR Mid-infrared

MTI Moving Target Indicator

NIR Near Infra Red

NVG Night Vision Goggles

OTIS Thermal imager

OP Observation Point

Para cord Strong thin cord

Poncho As worn by Clint Eastwood but with a hood

Radio Sensors Devices that pick up radio transmissions

Recce Abbreviated form of reconnaissance

Reconnaissance Checking out an area or target

RV Rendezvous or meeting place

ERV Emergency Rendezvous – a fall back meeting place

SAS Special Air Service – government hit squad

Spyglass A thermal imager

Stag Being on watch

Stand-off Keeping a distance

Stand-to Being in a high state of awareness

Surveillance Watching a target

Target An object or person that offends you

Terrorist (1) The State; (2) Someone not approved of by The State/Big Business

TIR Thermal-infrared

TI Thermal imaging

TADS A thermal imaging sight

UV Ultraviolet

Visual Sensors From the Mark 1 eyeball to the most sophisticated imaging technology

Useful Sources

NAVIGATION

- *Map Reading Made Easy*, useful free leaflet from Ordnance Survey
- *Mountaincraft and Leadership* by Eric Langmuir (3rd edition, ISBN 1850602956, published by MLTB/Sport Scotland, £14.99) – for the more advanced navigator
- *The Art of Outdoor Navigation* by Martyn Hurn (CD-ROM, produced by Outdoornav, £19.95)
- Virtually Hillwalking, produced by OS and SportScotland and free to download from the OS site
- *Hillwalking* by Steve Long (2nd revised edition, ISBN 0954151100, published by Mountain Leader Training UK, £14.99) – probably the best of these books

TECHNIQUES – WEB

www.atiam.train.army.mil (over 500 US military Field Manuals) useful ones include:

- FM 3-25.26 MAP READING AND LAND NAVIGATION probably needs to be read in conjunction with a civilian guide
- FM 3-25.150 COMBATIVES good self defence techniques
- FM 3-97.61 MILITARY MOUNTAINEERING
- FM 5-125 RIGGING
- FM 4-25.11 FIRST AID
- FM 31-70 BASIC COLD WEATHER MANUAL
- FM 31-71 NORTHERN OPERATIONS, photography section is good

These circulars from the above site are also good:

- TC 21-3 SOLDIER'S HANDBOOK FOR INDIVIDUAL OPERATIONS AND SURVIVAL IN COLD-WEATHER AREAS
- TC 21-24 RAPPELLING abseiling
- TC 25-20 A LEADER'S GUIDE TO AFTER-ACTION REVIEWS, cut through the jargon and the hierarchical nature of anything military and it could be of use for a debrief session

www.globalsecurity.org/military/library/policy/army – this link is good for some manuals which are not on the above site, including:

- FM 21-76-1 SURVIVAL, EVASION AND RECOVERY

TECHNIQUES – BOOKS

- *Rogue Male* by Geoffrey Household (ISBN 075285139X, published by Orion Trade) – this is a great novel and will teach you everything you could ever wish to know about living in a hedge!
- *Road Raging* (ISBN 0953185206, published by Road Alert)

- *The Complete Guide to Lock Picking* by Eddie the Wire (ISBN 0915179067, published by Loompanics Unlimited) – the title says it all. I would recommend you check out Loompanics for all your subversive reading needs
- *Ecodefence! – A Field Guide to Monkeywrenching* edited by Dave Foreman and Bill Haywood (3rd edition, ISBN 0963775103, published by Abbzug Press, 1993) – essential reading for monkey wrenching techniques
- *Ozymandias Sabotage Skills Handbook Volume 1 – Getting Started* by Anonymous (1st edition, no ISBN, self published, 1995) – check the web at: http://cafeunderground.com/Cafesite/Rooms/Ozymandia/sabotage_index.html http://www.reachoutpub.com/osh/
- *Road Raging – Top Tips for Wrecking Road Building* (2nd edition, no ISBN, published by Road Alert, 1998) Check the web at: http://www.eco-action.org/
- 'An Interview with an ALF Activist' in *Without a Trace* by Anonymous (self published pamphlet, no ISBN)
- *The ID Forger: Homemade Birth Certificates and Other Documents Explained* by John Q. Newman (ISBN 1559501960, published by Loompanics Unlimited, 1999)
- *Secrets of a Back Alley ID Man: Fake ID Construction Techniques of the Underground* by Sheldon Charrett (ISBN 1581602685, published by Paladin Press, 2001)
- *Survival Advantage* by Andrew Lane (no ISBN, published by Aegis Publishing, Nanholme Mill, Shaw Wood Road, Todmorden, West Yorkshire) – this is by far the best survival book I have read
- *How to Shit in the Woods* by Kathleen Meyer (ISBN 09891562-0, published by Ten Speed Press
- *Direct Action* by Ann Hansen (ISBN 1902593480, published by AK Press) – the trials and tribulations of a bunch of Canadian urban guerrillas, and incidentally a great how *not* to do it book

WEATHER
www.mwis.org.uk
www.metcheck.com
www.met-office.gov.uk
www.para-excellence.co.uk

TARGET RESEARCH
- *Doing Business* by by D. Spig (ISBN 0948994029, published by 1 in 12 Publications collective)
- *Written in Flames* (ISBN 1869802071, published by Hooligan Press)
- *The Investigative Researchers Handbook* by Stuart Christie (ISBN 0946222053, published by BCM Refract)

- http://www.cafeunderground.com
- Corporate Watch, www.corpwatch.org

FORENSICS
- *Without a Trace* – a must read but, as with the books above, things change very quickly and published stuff dates very quickly – use the net as much as possible for up to date information
- http://home.earthlink.net/~thekeither/Forensic/forsone.htm

EQUIPMENT
- www.usmcpro.com – army surplus kit
- www.henrykrank.com – alarm mines

Appendix i
The Phonetic Alphabet

The phonetic alphabet is used to spell letters rather than just saying the letter itself. By using a word for each letter there is less chance that the person listening will confuse letters. For instance, some letters than can easily be confused are 'b' and 'e'. The phonetic alphabet is used in radio communications around the world by maritime units, aircraft, amateur radio operators and the military.

Letter	Pronunciation
A	Alpha (AL fah)
B	Bravo (BRAH VOH)
C	Charlie (CHAR lee)
D	Delta (DELL tah)
E	Echo (ECK oh)
F	Foxtrot (FOKS trot)
G	Golf (GOLF)
H	Hotel (hoh TELL)
I	India (IN dee ah)
J	Juliet (JEW lee ETT)
K	Kilo (KEY loh)
L	Lima (LEE mah)
M	Mike (MIKE)
N	November (no VEM ber)
O	Oscar (OSS cah)
P	Papa (pah PAH)
Q	Quebec (keh BECK)
R	Romeo (ROW me oh)
S	Sierra (see AIR rah)
T	Tango (TANG go)
U	Uniform (YOU nee form)
V	Victor (VIK tah)
W	Whiskey (WISS key)

X   **X Ray (ECKS RAY)**

Y   **Yankee (YANG key)**

Z   **Zulu (ZOO loo)**

Note: The syllables printed in capital letters are to be stressed.

Example: "My name is Crowbar – Charlie, Romeo, Oscar, Whiskey, Bravo, Alpha, Romeo."

Use the phonetic alphabet when radios conditions are less then perfect or the other party often says, 'What' or 'Say again', or 'ten, nine'.

Appendix ii
Equipment

NIGHT VISION

With the proper night-vision equipment, you can see a person standing over 200 yards (183m) away on a moonless, cloudy night!

Night vision can work in two very different ways, depending on the technology used.

- Image enhancement: This works by collecting the tiny amounts of light, including the lower portion of the infrared light spectrum, that are present but may be imperceptible to our eyes, and amplifying it to the point that we can easily observe the image.
- Thermal imaging: This technology operates by capturing the upper portion of the infrared light spectrum, which is emitted as heat by objects instead of simply reflected as light. Hotter objects, such as warm bodies, emit more of this light than cooler objects like trees or buildings.

In order to understand night vision, it is important to understand something about light. The amount of energy in a light wave is related to its wavelength: shorter wavelengths have higher energy. Of visible light, violet has the most energy and red has the least. Just next to the visible light spectrum is the infrared spectrum.

Infrared light can be split into three categories:

- Near-infrared (near-IR): Closest to visible light, near-IR has wavelengths that range from 0.7 to 1.3 microns, or 700 billionths to 1,300 billionths of a metre.
- Mid-infrared (mid-IR): Mid-IR has wavelengths ranging from 1.3 to 3 microns. Both near-IR and mid-IR are used by a variety of electronic devices, including remote controls.
- Thermal-infrared (thermal-IR): Occupying the largest part of the infrared spectrum, thermal-IR has wavelengths ranging from 3 microns to over 30 microns.

The key difference between thermal-IR and the other two is that thermal-IR is emitted by an object instead of reflected off it. Infrared light is emitted by an object because of what is happening at the atomic level.

THERMAL IMAGING

Here's how thermal imaging works: a special lens focuses the infrared light emitted by all of the objects in view.

The focused light is scanned by a phased array of infrared-detector elements. The detector elements create a very detailed temperature pattern called a thermogram. It only takes about one-thirtieth of a second for the detector array to obtain the temperature information to make the thermogram. This information is obtained from several thousand points in the field of view of the detector array.

The thermogram created by the detector elements is translated into electric impulses.

The impulses are sent to a signal-processing unit, a circuit board with a dedicated chip that translates the information from the elements into data for the display.

The signal-processing unit sends the information to the display, where it appears as various colours depending on the intensity of the infrared emission. The combination of all the impulses from all of the elements creates the image.

TYPES OF THERMAL IMAGING DEVICES

Most thermal-imaging devices scan at a rate of 30 times per second. They can sense temperatures ranging from -4 degrees Fahrenheit (-20 degrees Celsius) to 3,600°F (2,000°C), and can normally detect changes in temperature of about 0.4°F (0.2°C) There are two common types of thermal-imaging devices:

- **Un-cooled**: This is the most common type of thermal-imaging device. The infrared-detector elements are contained in a unit that operates at room temperature. This type of system is completely quiet, activates immediately and has the battery built right in.

- **Cryogenically cooled**: More expensive and more susceptible to damage from rugged use, these systems have the elements sealed inside a container that cools them to below 32°F (zero°C). The advantage of such a system is the incredible resolution and sensitivity that result from cooling the elements. Cryogenically-cooled systems can 'see' a difference as small as 0.2°F (0.1°C) from more than 1,000ft (300m) away, which is enough to tell if a person is holding a gun at that distance!

While thermal imaging is great for detecting people or working in near-absolute darkness, most night-vision equipment uses image-enhancement technology, which you will learn about in the next section.

ENHANCEMENT

Image-enhancement technology is what most people think of when you talk about night vision. In fact, image-enhancement systems are normally called night-vision devices (NVDs). NVDs rely on a special tube, called an image-intensifier tube, to collect and amplify infrared and visible light.

Here's how image enhancement works: a conventional lens, called the objective lens, captures ambient light and some near-infrared light.

The gathered light is sent to the image-intensifier tube. In most NVDs, the power supply for the image-intensifier tube receives power from two N-Cell or two 'AA' batteries. The tube outputs a high voltage, about 5,000 volts, to the image-tube components.

The image-intensifier tube has a photocathode, which is used to convert the photons of light energy into electrons.

As the electrons pass through the tube, similar electrons are released from atoms in the tube, multiplying the original number of electrons by a factor of thousands through the use of a microchannel plate (MCP) in the tube. An MCP is a tiny, glass disc that has millions of microscopic holes (microchannels) in it, made using fiber-optic technology. The MCP is contained in a vacuum and has metal electrodes on either side of the disc. Each channel is about 45 times longer than it is wide, and it works as an electron multiplier.

The green phosphor image is viewed through another lens, called the ocular lens, which allows you to magnify and focus the image. The NVD may be connected to an electronic display, such as a monitor, or the image may be viewed directly through the ocular lens.

When the electrons from the photo cathode hit the first electrode of the MCP, they are accelerated into the glass microchannels by the 5,000v bursts being sent between the electrode pair. As electrons pass through the microchannels, they cause thousands of other electrons to be released in each channel.

GENERATIONS

NVDs have been around for more than 40 years. They are categorised by generation. Each substantial change in NVD technology establishes a new generation.

- **Generation 0**: The original night-vision system created by the United States Army and used in World War II and the Korean War, these NVDs use active infrared. This means that a projection unit, called an IR Illuminator, is attached to the NVD. The unit projects a beam of near-infrared light, similar to the beam of a normal flashlight. Invisible to the naked eye, this beam reflects off objects and bounces back to the lens of the NVD. These systems use an anode in conjunction with the cathode to accelerate the electrons. The problem with that approach is that the acceleration of the electrons distorts the image and greatly decreases the life of the tube. Another major problem with this technology in its original military use was that it was quickly duplicated by hostile nations, which allowed enemy soldiers to use their own NVDs to see the infrared beam projected by the device.
- **Generation 1**: The next generation of NVDs moved away from active infrared, using passive infrared instead. Once dubbed Starlight by the U.S. Army, these NVDs use ambient light provided by the moon and stars to augment the normal amounts of reflected infrared in the environment. This means that they do not require a source of projected infrared light. This also means that they do not work very well on cloudy or moonless nights. Generation-1 NVDs use the same image-intensifier tube technology as Generation 0, with both cathode and anode, so image distortion and short tube life are still a problem.

- **Generation 2**: Major improvements in image-intensifier tubes resulted in Generation 2 NVDs. They offer improved resolution and performance over Generation 1 devices, and are considerably more reliable. The biggest gain in Generation 2 is the ability to see in extremely low light conditions, such as a moonless night. This increased sensitivity is due to the addition of the microchannel plate to the image-intensifier tube. Since the MCP actually increases the number of electrons instead of just accelerating the original ones, the images are significantly less distorted and brighter than earlier-generation NVDs.
- **Generation 3**: Generation 3 is currently used by the U.S. military. While there are no substantial changes in the underlying technology from Generation 2, these NVDs have even better resolution and sensitivity. This is because the photo cathode is made using gallium arsenide, which is very efficient at converting photons to electrons. Additionally, the MCP is coated with an ion barrier, which dramatically increases the life of the tube.
- **Generation 4**: What is generally known as Generation 4 or "filmless and gated" technology shows significant overall improvement in both low- and high-level light environments. The removal of the ion barrier from the MCP that was added in Generation 3 technology reduces the background noise and thereby enhances the signal to noise ratio. Removing the ion film actually allows more electrons to reach the amplification stage so that the images are significantly less distorted and brighter. The addition of an automatic gated power supply system allows the photocathode voltage to switch on and off rapidly, thereby enabling the NVD to respond to a fluctuation in lighting conditions in an instant. This capability is a critical advance in NVD systems, in that it allows the NVD user to quickly move from high-light to low-light (or from low-light to high-light) environments without any halting effects. For example, consider the ubiquitous movie scene where an agent using night vision goggles is "sightless" when someone turns on a light nearby. With the new, gated power feature, the change in lighting wouldn't have the same impact; the improved NVD would respond immediately to the lighting change.

EQUIPMENT
Night-vision equipment can be split into three broad categories:
- **Scopes**: Normally handheld or mounted on a weapon, scopes are monocular (one eye-piece). Since scopes are handheld, not worn like goggles, they are good for when you want to get a better look at a specific object and then return to normal viewing conditions.
- **Goggles**: While goggles can be handheld, they are most often worn on the head. Goggles are binocular (two eye-pieces) and may have a single lens or stereo lens, depending on the model. Goggles are excellent for constant viewing, such as

moving around in a dark building. Detectives and private investigators use night vision to watch people they are assigned to track. Many businesses have permanently-mounted cameras equipped with night vision to monitor the surroundings.

A really amazing ability of thermal-imaging is that it reveals whether an area has been disturbed – it can show that the ground has been dug up to bury something, even if there is no obvious sign to the naked eye. Law enforcement has used this to discover items that have been hidden by criminals, including money, drugs and bodies. Also, recent changes to areas such as walls can be seen using thermal imaging, which has provided important clues in several cases.

• **Cascaded secondary emission:** Basically, the original electrons collide with the side of the channel, exciting atoms and causing other electrons to be released. These new electrons also collide with other atoms, creating a chain reaction that results in thousands of electrons leaving the channel where only a few entered. An interesting fact is that the microchannels in the MCP are created at a slight angle (about a 5-degree to 8-degree bias) to encourage electron collisions and reduce both ion and direct-light feedback from the phosphors on the output side.

At the end of the image-intensifier tube, the electrons hit a screen coated with phosphors. These electrons maintain their position in relation to the channel they passed through, which provides a perfect image since the electrons stay in the same alignment as the original photons. The energy of the electrons causes the phosphors to reach an excited state and release photons. These phosphors create the green image on the screen that has come to characterise night vision.

Appendix iii
Forensics

TOOL MARK IDENTIFICATION

For example, your new trainers will have the same tread pattern as all the other trainers of that brand. These are class characteristics. Individual characteristics are those characteristics which are unique to a given object and set it apart from similar objects. When you have worn your trainers for a while they get worn. The treads wear down. They get little pits and gouges in them. These little pits and gouges are individual to your shoes and no others, since no one has walked over the exact same surfaces in the exact same way.

IMPRINT EVIDENCE

There are two basic types of imprint evidence. Three dimensional impressions, in which an object presses into something soft which retains the impression of that object; and two dimensional impressions, in which an object transfers an image to a surface or an object comes into contact with a surface that is coated and removes some of that coating.

An example of a 3D impression is someone stepping into mud. The mud hardens as it dries and retains the print.

An example of the first type of 2D print would be the step after you've stepped into spilled paint. The paint coats the bottom of your shoe when you step in it. It is then transferred to another surface when you step down. It is just like using a rubber ink stamp.

An example of the second type of 2D imprint is when you stepped into the paint. You removed some of the paint, creating a negative image of the bottom of your shoe in the paint spill.

Wheel base is the distance between the two front wheels and the distance between the front and rear wheels. These distances have been charted and can be used to narrow down the make of the car. The tread design itself, as discussed above, can narrow down the list of possible cars. The police maintain books that contain images of every type of tyre imprint, just for this purpose. The individual wear, developed from use, will show up in the impression, allowing for identification of a single car, to the exclusion of all others. They can also tell which way the car was facing, how they pulled out and in what direction.

HANDWRITING ANALYSIS

Every person develops unique peculiarities and characteristics in their handwriting. Handwriting analysis looks at letter formations, connecting strokes between the letters, upstrokes, retraces, down strokes, spacing, baseline, curves, size, distortions, hesitations and a number of other characteristics of handwriting. By examining these details and variations in a questioned sample and comparing them to a sample of known authorship, a determination can be made as the whether or not the authorship is genuine.

PHOTOCOPIERS AND LASER PRINTERS

Photocopiers and laser printers use the same type of process to print a page. With a photocopier, the original document is placed on the glass platen. The document is then exposed by use of reflected light to a drum that is covered with a photosensitive material. The image of that document exists on the drum as an invisible, positive photoelectric charge. Negatively charged toner, the messy black powdery stuff, is drizzled onto the drum, where it sticks to only the positively charged areas, to create a visible image. Paper, with a positive charge, passes the drum, causing the negatively charged toner to transfer to the paper. The toner is then heat sealed to the paper, creating the printed copy. With a laser printer, the image of the original document (held by the computer in its memory) is written to the photosensitive drum by use of a laser. There are many ways to match a page back to a photocopier or laser printer. Since, as shown above, the processes are similar, the methods used to match a page back to its origin, printer or copier, will also be similar. The paper itself can yield many clues. Look for marks from the belts, pinchers, rollers and gears that physically move the paper through a machine. These examinations would be similar to tool mark examinations. Toner can have unique characteristics in its chemical composition. Also, look at how the toner was placed on and fused to the paper. Toner may clump up on the drum, transferring blobs of toner at a time to the printed page. Marks on the optics (glass platen, lenses, mirrors) used to transfer or create an image on paper might contain unique defects (such as scratches) that will render anomalous markings on the printed page.

FORGERY

Forgery, particularly of ID cards, is something you will probably get into at some time. There are four basic types of forgery: traced, simulation, freehand and lifted.

There are a few different ways to do traced forgeries: with overlays (as with tracing paper), transmitted light (as with a light box), tracing the indentations left in the page underneath the original writing, and tracing patterns of dots that outline the writing to be forged. Simulation involves the copying of writing from a genuine article; trying to imitate the handwriting of the original. Freehand forgeries are written with no knowledge of the appearance of the original; just writing off the top of your head and passing it off as something else. The final type is a lifted forgery, in which tape is used to lift off a signature, and then place it on another document. Freehand forgeries are the easiest to detect. Simulation forgeries are easy to detect for a number of reasons. It is very difficult to copy another's handwriting. The style will not be as fluid because the writing does not come naturally. Consequently, the forged writing will show tremors, hesitations and other variations in letter quality that 'comfortable' handwriting would not have. Traced forgeries and lifts are easy enough to detect, but the identity of the forger cannot be determined.

COUNTERFEIT SECURITY MEASURES

Part of the reason why US currency is being redesigned is simply because it is so easy to make fakes. According to an article in the The Observer, computer and software manufacturers in Europe are to be forced to introduce new security measures to make it impossible for their products to be used to copy banknotes.

The latest version of Adobe Photoshop, a popular graphics package, already generates an error message if the user attempts to scan banknotes of main currencies. A number of printer manufactures have also incorporated the software so that only an inch or so of a banknote will reproduce.

The software relies on features built into leading currencies. Latest banknotes contain a pattern of five tiny circles. On the euro notes they appear in a constellation of stars. Imaging software or devices detect the pattern and refuse to deal with the image.

PERSONAL IDENTIFICATION

Fingerprints
There are three basic fingerprint patterns: Loops, Arches and Whorls. Everyone falls into one of these three patterns. Within these patterns are minutiae points. There are about thirty different types of minutiae points, and no two people have the same types of minutiae in the same number in the same places on their fingertips. This is why our fingerprints are totally unique. Your fingerprint patterns are hereditary. They are formed before you

are born, while you are still in the womb, they never change through out your lifetime, and they are even around for a while after you die. Your fingerprints are formed underneath your skin in a layer called dermal ateriel. As long as that layer of ateriel is there, your fingerprints will always come back, even after scarring or burning.

Different surfaces require different techniques for developing prints. In the movies, you usually see detectives with brushes. They are powder processing the prints. Minute particles of powder cling to the print residue as the brush passes over it. The print is then lifted with tape. Another process involves fuming. Vapours of iodine and superglue (bonds in seconds) will coalesce inside the print residue to reveal a latent print. There are special processes that develop prints on paper, wood and cardboard. Fingerprints can be developed on objects that have been in water. Prints can be developed off of skin (such as from the neck of a strangulation victim). There are very few surfaces on which a print cannot be developed. Computers have revolutionised the techniques used to match fingerprints. Until recently, the old standard was the Henry Classification System – a cumbersome sequence of letters and numbers broken down into several levels of classification. It could take weeks, sometimes months to compare a suspect fingerprint to a department's print files. The advent of digital technology has changed all of that. Prints can be image scanned directly into a computer, doing away with ink and fingerprint cards. Prints can be compared at a rate of 400,000 per second. It's called AFIS. Automated Fingerprint Identification System. Departments will input all the prints from arrests and all of the print cards they already have on file to create an historical record. They also input all of the prints from any unsolved crimes, in the hope that a hit might come up from a routine arrest. Local departments are linking their systems into a national database.

DNA

DNA is constructed like a ladder – a ladder that has been grabbed at both ends and twisted, creating the double helix shape. The rails of the ladder are phosphate and sugar groups. They link together (sugar+phosphate+sugar+phosphate) to form the backbone. There are four bases that form the rungs of the ladder: Cytocene, Guanine, Thiamine and Adnine. They are always in pairs and always complement each other; Cytocene is always paired with Guanine and Thiamine is always paired with Adnine. Each base forms half of the rung, meeting in the middle. Now, think of that ladder as a zip. When DNA replicates, is unzips down the middle, separating the base pairs like a zip. The complementary bases now attach to the opened segments to make new DNA. One DNA analysis technique looks at junk DNA. Everybody's DNA is pretty similar. Everyone who has blue eyes has pretty much the same code for blue eyes. Everyone who has brown hair has pretty much the same code for brown hair. But these coding sequences are separated by 'junk' DNA. This 'junk' DNA is non-coding and only serves to separate the coding sequences. These 'junk' DNA sequences are totally random and totally unique to an individual. The process is extremely technical, but that is the concept, and it's really not that hard to understand.

FORENSIC PHOTOGRAPHY

What items are photographed at a crime scene? Bullet casings – photograph as a group and photograph individually. Photograph any dropped items, foot prints or animal tracks. Photograph any tool marks, bite marks or skin impressions. Basically, anything that might be evidence is photographed.

Imprint evidence requires extra measures. Shoe imprints are photographed individually and as a series or group. Shoe imprints need to be lit from the side to show as much detail in the imprint as possible. Tyre imprints are photographed from above as a whole. If the tyre imprint is four feet long, then a picture showing all four feet is taken. Detail pictures are then taken showing one foot sections, each picture overlapping the one before it. This way, specific detail can be shown and the overlapping pictures lined up to show the whole print. Again, all pictures are taken with and without a scale.

SOIL

Typical collection sites include shoes, tyres, pedals, carpeting and wheel wells on cars. Soil characteristics vary with geographic location. Soil found out of its native geographical area can be matched back to its area of origination.

GLASS

Class characteristics of glass include its colour, thickness and refractive index (how much it bends the light that passes through it), and whether it is flat or curved. There may be a drug or liquid residue on the glass or even footprints if the glass if found on the floor.

Glass breaks in a characteristic manner which indicates the direction of travel of the impacting object. Conchoidal striations are ripples seen through the cross section of broken glass. They are always at right angles to the impacted surface. The radial cracks will stop where an earlier crack already exists, so it must have come later in the sequence.